Live a more fulfilling life …

Let go of stress, fear, and worry..

Discover the love, joy, and peace that you have
been seeking.

SPIRITUALITY FOR EFFECTIVE LIVING

*What you hold in your hands is not simply a book of ideas. It is a living current
of awareness flowing through the words, inviting you to enter a sacred relationship
with your own inner being. … Born from Govind's [Marty's] own journey of
transformation, this book carries the imprint of sincere inner practice and the
living presence that unfolds from it.*

— **SRI AMRITJI (YOGI AMRIT DESAI)**, internationally
renowned authority in the field of Yoga

*This book is a gem! Its spiritual teachings are both profound and practical, the
kind that can open your heart and change your life. Each chapter shines a light on
a different area of life, offering simple, powerful ways to live with more joy and
fulfillment. Read it, reread it, and share it with everyone you love.*

— **MARCI SHIMOFF**, #1 New York Times best-selling author of
Happy for No Reason and *Chicken Soup for the Woman's Soul*

Practical, grounded, and powerfully effective—Marty's **Spirituality for
Effective Living** *offers a refreshing approach to inner work. Instead of telling
you what to believe, it shows you how to transform your experience from the inside*

out. *I recommend it to anyone ready to deepen their practice and truly change their life.*

—**BENJAMIN W. DECKER**, author of *Modern Spirituality* and *Practical Meditation for Beginners*

This book is a gentle yet powerful guide to discovering spirituality without dogma or religion. Rooted in meditation and years of shared talks, Govind lovingly invites you to explore peace, joy, and inner knowing through simple, practical reflections. Each well-written chapter offers accessible teachings that resonate differently at different times, encouraging you to experiment and find what feels true. It is a profound companion for anyone seeking more meaning, fulfillment, and love in daily life. It is easy to read and hard not to be inspired!!!

—**PEGGY SEALFON**, BCHC, award-winning author of *Awakening: A Novel*, lifestyle coach, and creator of the Mind Body Fitness for Life system

Spirituality for Effective Living *is inspired and powerful. You are drawn in by the relatable examples, but what you are drawn into is profound and potentially life changing. Marty clearly describes the limitations most of us live with and the joyful, peaceful, loving life that is available to each one of us—now.*

—**Stephen Cope**, Award winning and bestselling author of *The Great Work of Your Life*

Spirituality for Effective Living

Teachings of the Masters Through an Unenlightened Disciple

Marty Simon EdD

Publisher's Note

This book was written to provide useful information in regard to the subject matter. It provides no professional services. If professional assistance or counseling is needed, a competent professional should be engaged.

ISBN-979-8-9933379-1-3

Contents

Foreword

What you hold in your hands is not simply a book of ideas. It is a living current of awareness flowing through the words, inviting you to enter a sacred relationship with your own inner being. As you read, do not try to understand with the mind alone. Instead, let the words draw you inward, where you may discover what has always been waiting in the stillness of your own presence. Born from Govind's own journey of transformation, this book carries the imprint of sincere inner practice and the living presence that unfolds from it. This writing is not for your intellect. It is a call to your essence.

The true purpose of spiritual practice is not to change what you experience, but to awaken the one who is experiencing. In this recognition, all doing dissolves into being, and the seeker merges with the truth that was never absent. You may think you are reading this book to gain something new, but what it truly offers is a return to what you have forgotten, to what was lost not in reality but in your identification with memory, fear, and striving. This is not a path of becoming. It is the pathless path of remembering who you are.

Spiritual awakening begins not with effort but with sincerity. The sincere desire to know yourself beyond your mind opens a doorway to the sacred. That doorway is here now. It opens each time you witness a thought without grasping, feel an emotion without resistance, and rest in the present moment without reaching for something else. When you turn within, you step out of the prison of the past and awaken to the infinite that is already alive in you. This is not philosophy. It is direct experience, available now.

In one moment of openness, your suffering begins to dissolve. I remember when Govind came to me many years ago, not just seeking answers but longing for direct experience. That longing has now flowered into this offering. What he shares here does not come from accumulated knowledge. It comes from deep inner work, from choosing presence over reaction, and from the courage to feel what most people run from. May this book guide you in the same way, not to somewhere else, but to the Now where you have never been separate from your Self.

Gurudev Shri Amritji

Amrit Desai is the developer of Kripalu Yoga, founder of Kripalu Yoga Centers, and originator of I AM Yoga (Amrit Yoga Institute), now based in Salt Springs, Florida

**http://www.amritji.tv https://www.amritji.org
https://amrityoga.org**

Acknowledgements

I have been blessed with great teachers and life-changing teachings. I first want to acknowledge my guru, Yogi Amrit Desai. On Thanksgiving morning, 1990, I was not looking for a spiritual teacher, but indeed I found one. Thank you for the many years of love, support, and teachings. I hope this book shows you the impact that you have had on me. You have taught me that as a disciple I further my own spiritual development through teaching and service. Jai Gurudev!

Mickey Singer, you have been a very important teacher to me. You express the teachings so clearly that it is difficult to miss their meaning. Thank you!

Courtney Pierce, you have been my spiritual counselor since 2014 nurturing my spiritual unfolding throughout these years. I am so grateful for your love and guidance.

To my family–particularly my parents (deceased), my daughter Alyssa and her family, and my partner Nicola–and to my friends, thank you for your love and unwavering support.

Thank you to my dear friend and colleague, Doug Clements, for proofreading the manuscript. I am glad we are walking this path together.

Finally, thanks to the members of my meditation group. Without you, this book would not have happened. Your commitment to your own spiritual development and your presence in the group has contributed to drawing out the teachings that have come through me.

With gratitude, love, and respect.
Marty

Introduction

This book is an accessible, practical guide for using spirituality to live a more fulfilling life. Making use of this book requires no particular beliefs. It has no connection to any particular religion or to religion in general. I have chosen not to refer to "God" or any deities. Readers are free to make such connections themselves (or not). Thus, these teachings are available to people of all religions and no religion.

The chapters that follow derive from talks I have given over the last few years in the meditation group that I lead online. The group is open and free of charge to all.

My Spiritual Background

Up until Thanksgiving 1990, I had no conscious experience of spirituality. That Thanksgiving Day, I heard a talk by Yogi Amrit Desai, and my spiritual journey began in earnest. Over the next three years, I attended a number of his talks and retreats, and in October 1993, I became a disciple of Yogi Desai and received the Sanskrit name Govind.

Through Yogi Desai ("Gurudev"), I met Michael (Mickey) Singer, who became an important spiritual teacher for me. I heard him speak several times at Temple of the Universe, listened to his recorded talks, and read his books.

About 10 years ago, I began leading a meditation group in New York City. Shortly after moving to Colorado in 2020, I began leading an online meditation group. Every group session begins with a 20-minute silent meditation. I then give a short talk, which is followed by questions and discussion.

My Meditation-Group Talks

In my career as a professor of education and educational researcher, I have given many lectures about my work. I learned to prepare and deliver these lectures effectively. However, I want my spiritual talks to be different–to not be the product of my rational mind. I see myself as a conduit for teachings that come through me. To respect this process, I do no preparation for the talks. I usually have a topic in mind. I am always excited to receive and share the teachings. I learn as much as anyone as these talks unfold.

This Book

Why did I write this book? First, the group and I have benefitted greatly from the teachings that have come through during our meditation group sessions. The teachings are powerful, and it became clear that they should be made more widely available. Second, as an "unenlightened disciple", my expression of these teachings might make them accessible to the typical reader. Third, my career as an educator has honed my ability to write while keeping in mind the readers' understanding. Writing this book is not just about sharing the teachings; it is about helping the reader progress in their knowing and awareness.

The book consists of short chapters, each of which can be read easily in one sitting. Each chapter focuses on spirituality in a different aspect of our lives. Words are an inadequate (albeit essential) medium for capturing spirituality. There are not a multitude of spiritual messages. However, discussing spirituality in a diversity of contexts gives us multiple opportunities to grasp, practice, and apply the spiritual teachings.

Relationship to the Teachings I have Received

Without the teachings I have received, this book and the meditation-group talks would not exist. As I indicated, I have benefited greatly from the teachings of Yogi Amrit Desai and Mickey Singer. However, this book presents the teachings as they came through me. They are *not* a repetition or paraphrase of the words of my teachers. That said, the teachings that I share here are consistent with the teachings of Gurudev and Mickey. Their love and teachings have fashioned the conduit that I am. However, this book is a unique communication of the spiritual teachings.

Reading the Book

My advice to the reader is the same as it would be for any situation in which one listens to or reads spiritual teachings. Bring an openness. Many of us are great debaters and critics. However, those are not the qualities needed when encountering spiritual teachings. What is needed is a commitment to gleaning what you can. You will intuitively recognize some of what you read as true. It will resonate with your inner knowing. The rest you can let pass. Should you read the book (or individual chapters) again at a different time, other aspects of the teachings will resonate.

In this book, I do not ask you to adopt any beliefs. Rather, I invite you to experiment, and I offer discussion about why particular experiments might be worth engaging in.

Enjoy the book. May it support you in opening to more peace, joy, and love.

Marty/Govind

CHAPTER 1

What is Spirituality?

Spirituality is not religion. There is a fundamental difference between spirituality and religion. Religion generally requires adopting a set of beliefs, whereas spirituality does not. Furthermore, spirituality does not require belief in God or any deity.

So, what is spirituality? I consider spirituality to be a *personal science of living*. Let me explain why I call it a science. Spirituality is about looking at our experience of life and beginning to know what works and what doesn't work. It is about experimenting with different ways of interacting with life. It is about being curious, present, and aware.

What does it mean "to work?" It means that it provides us with what we really seek. Deep down, we all want the same things in our lives: joy, love, and peace. But don't people want to be rich, to be famous, to find a partner, to have a child or grandchild? Of course, people want these things, but why? They want them because they believe these things will bring them joy, love, or peace.

Each of us can practice spirituality on our own. However, there is great value in spiritual teachers and guides–people who have walked the path before us. Their role is not to tell us what to believe, because that is neither effective nor spiritual, but to draw our attention to aspects of our lives. We have become accustomed to the patterns and conditions of our lives. Spiritual teachers and teachings can help us recognize what we tend not to notice; they offer us a change in perspective.

So how does this process work? We start paying attention. We begin to notice that we are spending little time in a peaceful state. Rather, we are frequently stressed, fearful, and anxious. We are often in conflict with ourselves and others. We notice that we are seldom joyful. In many cases, we are just trying to be okay.

Why do we have fear? What's causing it? Fear is very practical when you are walking in the jungle and see a crocodile, or when you are walking down the street and somebody pulls a knife on you. Fear propels our fight or flight response, which can prevent physical harm or even save our lives. However, we rarely encounter physical threats, yet we spend considerable time experiencing fear.

We observe our fear and begin to see that the mind is creating a story about the future, and that story is provoking fear. The mind is specifying what will happen and the consequences of what will happen. We believe the mind's story and react to it. These observations lead to the question: Can we change this fear-producing pattern?

Paying attention leads to another major observation. We notice that we are constantly busy trying to manage the events of our lives. We are trying to get and achieve many things and are trying to avoid many others in order to be okay or happy. We may be trying to achieve more success or receive more recognition, acceptance, and love from others. We may be trying to get a larger income or a new house. We may be trying to find a relationship or have a child. At the same time, we are busy trying to avoid disease, injury, and disability.

We are trying to resist aging. We are trying to ensure that we do not lose what we have in terms of money and possessions. We are trying to make sure that we do not lose people in our lives that we love or lose their love and respect. We are busy trying to get what we desire and avoid what we fear, and, as a result, we are stressed and anxious.

Further observation leads to noticing that we have been busy trying to control all of these factors for our whole lives, and it has *never* worked. Perhaps, we have had a feeling of happiness when particular events have occurred or when we have had a particular experience. Perhaps, we have felt peaceful in a particular situation. However, these states are brief, and then we are back to being busy, stressed, and anxious—trying to get more of what made us happy and avoid what promises to make us unhappy. We notice that despite all the time and energy we devote to getting what we desire and avoiding what we fear, life never conforms to our preferences.

We begin to inquire about the source of this long list of what we want or need and what we do not want or fear. We see that its source is our mind (sometimes with social support). We realize that if we are to live in a state of joy, peace, and love, we need to find an alternative to pursuing the mind's list. We begin to explore who we are that is aware of the mind. We wonder about the life we are capable of living.

This is the beginning of spirituality. The remaining chapters of this book address questions raised here and offer an exploration of who we are and how spirituality can engage us in effective living. Spirituality is about experiencing what we seek—peace, joy, and love— now and in every moment. And as discussed, spirituality requires no beliefs. It involves recognizing what we know to be true and practicing living based on those truths.

CHAPTER 2

The Unproductive Pursuit of Happiness

Much of what we do in life, we do to make ourselves happier. Sometimes we do things just to be okay. We expend a lot of energy every day in this pursuit. So, the question is, if we are so devoted to making ourselves happy, why do we often experience unhappiness? Why, after years of this pursuit, have we not become ecstatic beings?

Before we consider answers to these questions, let's dig into the basis for our attempts to be happy. Our judgments about what will make us happy or feel okay are based on our memories of what seemed to have produced that effect in the past. We use these memories to project what will make us happy in the future. Thus, we are attempting to recreate something similar to what we remember making us happy. Why doesn't this work?

When we try to create what we remember made us happy or okay, several outcomes may occur. Perhaps you remember having a wonderful dinner at a nearby restaurant. You go back to that restaurant and order the same dish, but this time it is not as good as you remember, or the service is not as good, or the restaurant is noisier. There is a good chance that your attempt to recreate that remembered happiness will not only be unsuccessful but may actually result in disappointment.

Imagine that you are feeling a little blah. You realize that the ice cream you really like is in the freezer. You eat a bowl of ice cream and enjoy it. But all too soon, the bowl is empty. So, in an attempt to extend the "happiness", you have another bowl. However, the second bowl does less for you than the first. This is the law of diminishing returns. You may even eat enough that you feel uncomfortably full–not the experience you were aiming for.

The most extreme outcome of trying to recreate your memory of happiness (or being okay) is addiction. Whether it involves alcohol, drugs, gambling, sex, or even chocolate, it starts by trying to recreate a memory of a prior state and then doing so repeatedly until our well-being depends on it. Even if we do not succumb to addiction, the outcomes we have been discussing are less than satisfactory, often fleeting, and may actually lead to unhappiness.

So far, we have been talking about attempts to recreate a single experience based on a memory. However, we spend each day trying to obtain and create all that we believe will make us happy, feel okay, or be comfortable, while also avoiding all that we believe will make us unhappy. We are continually busy trying to control all the factors that we think will affect our happiness. The job is overwhelming and creates several problems. First, we never succeed. We never reach a point at which everything is just the way we want or need. Thus, we never achieve the envisioned happiness or dispel the fear of unhappiness. Second, this constant struggle to control creates stress.

Consider the following: You have been eagerly looking forward to your vacation. You anticipate a relaxing and enjoyable trip ("ah, happiness"). However, you end up creating stress because you have a conception of how things need to be on the vacation for you to be happy and relaxed. Perhaps the hotel room is not what you envisioned, the weather does not cooperate, or the food is not as advertised. Even on vacation, you are busy trying to be happy, but you cannot control all of the factors. Should it surprise us that we approach vacation the same way we approach the rest of life? You may be further stressed during your vacation because your wants and needs do not fit with those of others in your family or group. Perhaps you want a quiet evening sitting on the balcony, but your mate wants to explore the nightlife of this new locale. This creates conflict.

Another problem is that seeking happiness is focused on the future. *Seeking* implies finding or creating a condition that is not currently present. Seeking to be happy or okay in the future is an ongoing affirmation that we are not happy or okay now. We will be happy (okay) when ___ (fill in the blank). We are practicing not being okay, moment by moment. Continually practicing not being okay seems like a questionable way to become okay. Like anything else, what we practice, we perfect.

We have all kinds of conditions that we believe will make us happy or okay. "I'll be happy when I meet someone;" "I'll be okay when I get professional recognition;" "I'll be okay when I lose twenty pounds;" "I'll be happy when I retire." And what happens when we achieve the goal? Are we endlessly happy with no more fear, stress, or feelings of inadequacy? Of course not. Generally, we experience a brief period of positive feeling. Then we go back to normal, with fear, stress, and insecurity reigniting the search for what will bring us happiness. How many rich people seem to believe that they will be happy when they get even richer?

Another reason the pursuit of happiness fails is that the world exists in polarity—day and night, life and death, inhale and exhale. The mind attempts to split this polarity and create a duality, striving to get what it likes and avoid what it dislikes. But we never just get what we like. We never just get one half of the polarity. Heads always comes with tails. For example, if you meet someone and say, "This is the person who makes me happy, and I want to spend my life with this person," what comes with it is the fear of the person dying or leaving you. Along with the relationship that was to make you happy comes a new source of fear and worry. Everything intended to make us happy comes with what will make us unhappy.

So, does this discussion mean that we should not do things we enjoy? No, of course we do things we enjoy. When I go to the refrigerator, I take something out that I enjoy eating. When I plan an evening, I invite someone I enjoy being with. The question is, what is driving our choices? It is not the choice we make that is the problem; it is making choices for the purpose of being okay or being happy (in the future). There is an important difference between finishing a meal with a piece of chocolate and indulging in chocolate in an attempt to change our feeling of not being okay.

The whole enterprise of trying to be happy, okay, or relatively better is fraught with difficulties for all the reasons discussed. So, what is the alternative? To consider the alternative, we must engage in a key spiritual inquiry: "Who am I?" Up to this point in this chapter, I have referred to "you" and "we" as those who are pursuing happiness. However, the alternative to this unproductive pursuit requires each of us to recognize that I am not that entity. I am the consciousness. I am conscious of the mind's effort to seek happiness. Let's unpack this claim. The explicit part of the claim is that we are

11

consciousness, and the implicit part is that we are not the mind. This second part is important because most of us have spent our lives believing that we are the mind, identified with our thoughts and concepts. However, we also have experiences that suggest we are not our minds.

Can you relate to any of these experiences? "I have this song in my head that I cannot get rid of." "Since I saw that movie, I keep having scary thoughts." "My mind keeps going to that speech I am giving tomorrow." Who are *you*, the one who is aware of what is going on in your mind? The distinction between mind and consciousness is as simple as that. If I am aware of the mind, I am not the mind. I am the awareness, the consciousness.

Let's reflect on other experiences of ourselves as consciousness. You wake up in the morning and tell your partner, "I dreamt last night that…" Who knows that you had a dream and perhaps even the content of the dream? Not the mind that was dreaming, but the consciousness that was aware of the mind's engagement in a dream.

You looked in the mirror when you were five years old, fifteen years old, twenty-five years old, and continue to look in the mirror as you age. You see a different-looking face and body at each point in time. Yet there has been a continuity of self. "I saw myself at different ages." That "I" has remained constant, unchanging. At some level, we know ourselves as an unchanging being–as consciousness.

So, why is this important, and how is it related to the pursuit of happiness? It is the mind that engages in the unproductive pursuit of happiness. It is the mind that is busy trying to control all of the happiness and unhappiness factors it has identified from past experience. But if we are not the mind, we are not trapped in this ill-conceived enterprise. We can be aware of what the mind is telling us

("You will be okay/happy when …") and not buy into it. We can let those thoughts pass as if they are the advice of an unhelpful neighbor. By witnessing the mind, we let go of our identification with the mind–that is, we know that we are not the mind. This has two relevant effects. First, by letting go of the mind, we free ourselves from the unproductive pursuit of happiness. Second, when we let go of the mind, we know ourselves as consciousness, the being that is aware of the mind's activity. And *consciousness is inherently okay, joyful, and at peace in the present.*

Do we know anything about this last point? Consider times when you have been totally absorbed in the present moment. Perhaps you were looking at a beautiful landscape or engaged in a creative activity. Perhaps you were having a massage. Absorption in the present moment brings a quiet joy, a sense of well-being, and a sense of peace. Now think about the following. Have you ever felt a subtle (or not so subtle) wave of joy, a warm energy in your heart when nothing was happening externally to cause it? Most of us, if we pay attention, notice such experiences. These experiences reveal our potential to experience unprovoked joy at any, and therefore every, moment. When we are present, we are free of stress, anxiety, and fear of the future. We have dropped the overwhelming responsibility of trying to control life. We are not pursuing what we like while avoiding what we don't like. Therefore, we are not judging ourselves, others, or life events. We are present with what is, as it is. Free of fear, stress, and judgment, our hearts are open. The open heart allows a flow of joy and love. This is what we really seek.

The spiritual journey is about letting go of our identification with the mind and knowing ourselves as consciousness. Knowing ourselves as consciousness is always available. It does not require a particular setting, activity, or companion. The process of letting go of identification with the mind is as simple as witnessing it. When we witness the mind, we know we are not the mind, but rather the witness, the consciousness. When we witness the mind, we are present. Consider the following: You are feeling stressed about something that you believe will happen in the near future. However, at that moment, you notice the stress—the stressful thought that you are having and the concomitant tension in your body. In that instant, you shift from identifying with the stressed mind and body to knowing yourself as the consciousness, the witness of the stress. The mind that you are watching may take some time to relinquish its dialogue, and the body you are watching may take some time to release its stress. However, you, the consciousness, are not stressed even as you are witnessing stress. It is this simple transformation, in which we re-identify as the consciousness, that is available in every moment.

Although the process of returning to consciousness is simple, remaining conscious is not. Why? Because we have practiced identification with the mind for most of our lives. We have practiced following the mind's directives, including its impulse to pursue happiness. However, the more we practice witnessing the mind, the easier it becomes to let go of identification with the mind and remain conscious.

CHAPTER 3

Being Just Okay

W hen we meet someone, we know, we often ask, "How are you?" The responses are frequently, "I'm okay," "Not bad," or "Doing alright." These could be just common parlance, but they may also indicate that we have become accustomed to simply being "okay." What does it mean to be just okay? It likely means that nothing really bad is happening. We can develop, perhaps unconsciously, a sense that this is the goal, the way things should be and what we are trying to maintain. But isn't this a rather low bar? If we are honest with ourselves, it is not what we want. What we really want is to feel enthusiasm, energy, love, and peace. So, why do we set the bar so low?

We set the bar so low because, in the paradigm in which we are operating, "okay" is about as good as we can be for any significant period of time. Sure, we have peak experiences, but they are the exception and occur rarely. The paradigm in which most of us live is one in which we are identified with the ego mind.

The *ego mind* is the aspect of the mind that we mistakenly identify with. It is who we THINK WE ARE. It encompasses our thoughts about ourselves, including self-concept (see Chapter 17) and self-judgments (see Chapter 19). Our identification with the ego mind puts it in charge. As such, it is responsible for taking care of us.

The ego mind has only one way of taking care of us. It tries to manage everything that might affect us. It focuses on avoiding the things it believes will make us not okay and getting the things it believes will make us okay. As an aspect of mind, these beliefs are "learned." That is, they are based on the mind's memories of how particular situations affected us in the past.

Let's return to the issue of being just okay. Perhaps right now we are not hurting physically; we have people around us who care about us; we have a good job; and we can pay our bills. We are "okay" because nothing too disruptive is happening. At the same time, we are trying to maintain these things and fend off potential threats. However, the constant attempts to manage all the factors that can affect us put us in a state of constant stress. We take that level of stress as natural. Indeed, those around us are in the same condition.

However, as noted earlier, if we are really honest with ourselves, we realize that we crave something qualitatively different–a state in which we feel energy, love, and enthusiasm, and where we are free of fear and stress. The problem is, as long as the ego mind is in charge, we cannot do much better than "just okay." Although we take this condition as normal, deep down we are dissatisfied.

Let's take a trite, but relevant example of this dissatisfaction– the "midlife crisis." The midlife crisis is a spiritual crisis, although it is rarely identified as such. It is a point when we say to ourselves, "There has to be more to life than this!" Unfortunately, most people deal with the midlife crisis from the same paradigm that led to the crisis. They accept the solutions proposed by the ego mind–changes to their external conditions. They change jobs, have an affair, change partners, buy a fast car, or undergo cosmetic surgery. All of this is done in an effort to feel excitement and enthusiasm, to attract love, and to disrupt the unsatisfactory daily experience. Does it work? Perhaps temporarily–but temporarily is not a solution.

Do we have the potential for more than being just okay? If trying to control the world around us does not work, what is the alternative? Clearly, the ego mind cannot solve the problem it has created. The only potential for real change is to let go of our identity with the ego mind. When we witness the mind, we know that we are not the mind. We are the witness, the consciousness. Knowing that we are not the mind, we are free of its need to control external factors; thus, we are free of the stress this need creates. And free of that need, we are okay *now*, not sometime in the future dependent on the outcome of our struggle to control a myriad of factors. We are inherently and unconditionally okay. But this *okay* is different from the "just okay" that we have become accustomed to. This state is free of the stress we have considered natural and normal. Could this state be much greater than "okay?" Other writings and teachings describe this state in glowing terms. I will not try to describe it. Rather, I invite you to join me in the experiment of letting go of our identification with the ego mind and exploring the state we achieve by doing so.

But what does it mean to witness the ego mind? Let's take an example. The mind says, "I will be happy when I __ (lose weight, get a better job, meet someone …)." At that instant, we notice the mind's claim about our conditional happiness in the future and let it go. We do not fight with the mind. We just notice and let it go. At that moment, we are out. We are no longer run by the ego mind. At every moment, returning to the witness–the consciousness–is that simple and that available. And the more we do it, the more we become established in knowing ourselves as the consciousness.

We have lived for a long time in the old paradigm of identification with the ego mind. It is unlikely that we can drop that identification once and for all. The ego mind will slyly work its way back into control. Each time the ego mind regains control, we must remember and be willing to return to consciousness and witness the mind.

We do not have to leave our jobs, change partners, or buy expensive cars to have a more satisfying life. We just need to let go of who we are not, know that we are not the ego mind, and experiment with knowing ourselves as consciousness. In this state, being okay is not conditional upon external events. It is also not conditional on our emotions. Our emotions come and go. They can be positive and negative. We are the witness of these emotions. We are the consciousness.

CHAPTER 4

The Open Heart

One of the most wonderful experiences that we can have is the experience of an open heart. The experience of falling in love is a common experience of open-heartedness. Most people do not want the experience to end, and when they are not in love, they want to rekindle the experience. We like the experience because we feel love, joy, and enthusiasm running through us. We feel love not only for the person we are in love with, but for people we encounter, even strangers. Little things do not bother us. We have an incredible feeling of well-being. This is the condition of the open heart.

When my daughter was born, my heart was wide open for two or three days. Although very different, being with each of my parents as they took their final breaths was profoundly heart opening. The good news is that most of us have had experiences of having our hearts wide open. The bad news is that we do not have this experience often. It seems to only happen under special circumstances; we do not fall in love or have a baby all the time. The question is, can we have this experience more often? Can we have it without special circumstances?

Although the experience of having our hearts wide open is rare, having our hearts relatively open is not. Most of us open and close our hearts regularly. Minor events can trigger opening or closing. Perhaps you are out for dinner with a friend or loved one. You are feeling warm feelings; your heart is open. Then, your dinner partner says something that you perceive as critical, or the waiter gets your dinner order wrong, and your heart closes. Perhaps you are home feeling a little shut down. Your child calls to say he loves and misses you. Your heart opens. We take this opening and closing of the heart to be normal.

Although we love the experience of the open heart, most of us not only close our hearts but also justify doing so. Let's take an example: we have a conflict with somebody, and we're hurt, angry, frustrated, or disappointed. What does the mind say? It might say, "I have the right to be angry. She had no business talking to me that way. I'll show her—I won't talk to her." Not only have we closed our hearts, but our minds have reinforced this state by justifying it. Our minds assert that we are right to be in this condition—a condition that is opposite to what we really want. Would we rather be right or open-hearted?

We justify closing our hearts not only in interpersonal relationships but also in relation to current events. Many of us watch the news and are upset by the actions of political leaders—actions we consider insensitive, cruel, or discriminatory. Here too, we close our hearts and justify the closing. "Of course, I'm upset. Look at what's going on. What kind of person would I be if I wasn't upset and angry?" Are we making the world a better place by closing our hearts? We not only close our hearts, but our justifications keep our hearts closed. And yet we love having our hearts open.

Some of you may respond to the last example by saying, "If I don't get upset, I don't care." Keeping our hearts open and reopening

20

our hearts quickly when we close them does not mean we agree with or don't care about what is going on around us. We can still participate in what needs to be changed. Acting as an activist or agent of change does not require closing our hearts. In fact, what we do out of love, out of openness, is more likely to be appropriate and effective than what we do out of anger, frustration, and having a closed heart.

Gandhi demonstrated what it means to be an open-hearted activist. He was a key leader in the movement for India's independence from England. This included leading and participating in protests and demonstrations, some of which got him hit over the head with clubs. But my understanding is that he never closed his heart to the British. He kept his heart open and proceeded to do what he felt needed to be done, participating in the nonviolent overthrow of British rule. This is not to say that we can all be like Gandhi, but it does show us what is possible. If Gandhi can keep his heart open when getting hit by a club, then perhaps we have the ability to keep our hearts open or to reopen them quickly when we have a disagreement or don't like the way someone has spoken to us. Is it not worth exploring a more open-hearted way of living? We can be activists motivated by love rather than anger.

The mind will always be capable of justifying closing the heart. It can generate good reasons. This is part of its nature. Moreover, there is often social agreement for both closing and justifying. We can generally find allies who say, "You have every right to be angry," or "You are well within your rights to never speak to them again." However, if we genuinely want to experience open-heartedness more frequently, we must let go of both the internal and the external messages that justify closing. The question is, what is our intention?

Is our intention to justify closing our hearts and keeping our hearts closed, or is our intention to keep our hearts open as much as possible and to reopen when we reactively close?

So far, we have been discussing the opening and closing of the heart in response to common daily events. However, sometimes we experience deeply painful feelings, such as being left by a loved one. Some people respond to such experiences by either consciously or subconsciously deciding to close so that they cannot be hurt like that again. This is not wrong, but is it what we want? The heart is either open or closed. One cannot be open to love and closed to pain. It doesn't work that way. A window is either open or closed. If it's open, both hot air *and* cold air get in. If it's closed, neither gets in. It's the same way with the heart. We open our hearts, in which case we feel both love and pain, or we close our hearts and do not feel much of anything. This is an invitation for us to look at what we want.

A critical piece is knowing how to reopen the heart. It is inevitable that things will happen, and our hearts will close in reaction, but we do not need to remain in that reactive state. In Chapter 7, "Dealing with Uncomfortable Emotions," we will discuss a practice that can help us reopen our hearts.

CHAPTER 5

Nobody Is For You or Against You

Nobody is for you or against you. Really? Let's explore this claim.

When an event that has been planned for a long time gets canceled because of bad weather, some people take it personally. They feel that nature is against them. Of course, nature did not single them out. Atmospheric conditions produced the rain. Other people appreciate the rain; it waters their gardens or gives them a day off from work. The rain affects people in different ways, but the event itself is not personal. Nature has awesome power to create both beauty and devastation, to sustain life and to destroy life, but it is never personal.

The impersonal nature of natural events is easily grasped, but how about the actions of people? People are also capable of wonderful and destructive acts. Somebody could attack us verbally or physically. Are they *against* us? Somebody could say something supportive or do something helpful. Are they *for* us? We think people are for or against us because we consider people to have agency. Although we may be injured by a person or by nature, our minds say that people make choices; nature does not. Thus, it seems that people are capable of choosing to do something for or against us. We easily find evidence supporting this conclusion in both major and minor acts.

What do we usually mean when we say that people are for us or against us? We mean that they are acting in ways that align or do not align with our expectations about how they should behave toward us. Where do those expectations come from? We make them up. "They shouldn't talk to me that way." "They should help me." "They should remember my birthday." "They should be honest with me." Some of our expectations may have considerable social agreement and even legal support. But let's be honest, we pick and choose; our expectations are not always consistent with the majority view or the law.

So, we have made up a set of expectations, and they are the criteria by which we determine if people are for us or against us. In fact, it's not hard for somebody we consider to be for us to later be seen as against us. People get married, and then they get divorced, get in a relationship and break up. That person was for us, and now they are against us. But *for us* and *against us* is a function of our expectations.

People act in a variety of ways. I think everybody, if they had a choice, would act peacefully. They would be loving, kind, and giving. Living with an open heart is the most exquisite way to live. Who wouldn't want to live that way? Who would say, "No, I want to be somebody who walks around angry and punches people out." I don't think anybody would choose that if they had a *real* choice. But doesn't everybody have a choice? Do you have a choice? Do you always act in a kind, loving, generous way? If not, why not?

Let's consider two examples that are somewhat out of the norm and then turn to more common examples. If somebody were really drunk, and they came up to you in a bar and insulted you, and then they hit you, would you say that person is against you? Would you consider that person to have made a *choice* to interact with you in this manner? More likely, you would say, "They're really drunk. They have no control over what they are doing." You might say, "It's the alcohol talking." If somebody is schizophrenic, hallucinating, and starts screaming at or about you, you would likely say, "They're mentally ill, they can't help how they are behaving."

Now let's consider people who are not over the line of what we consider drunk or insane. First, let's observe that the line we draw between those we consider to be mentally impaired and those we consider to be responsible for their actions is arbitrary and perhaps somewhat fuzzy. Even the courts struggle with where to draw the line. But what about all of us who are "responsible" for our actions? As we acknowledged earlier, we do not always act in loving, kind, generous ways. In fact, we all have acted in inconsiderate and hurtful ways. Why?

The truth is that we have less choice than we realize; *our level of choice is a function of our level of consciousness*. Let's unpack this claim. Consider someone who has been feeling neglected by his spouse. His actions reflect these feelings in different ways. He might withhold affection, respond sharply, or make critical comments. Now consider a mom who is surprised and upset by something her child has done. She responds harshly, saying something hurtful. Did the people in these two examples have a choice? I argue that they probably did not.

All of us accumulate unfinished business, experiences that we have not fully processed. Our unfinished business gets reactivated by a subsequent event, causing a reaction that is not just a reaction to the new event. As such, it is disproportionate to the triggering event. We

25

do not choose these reactions. They may be reactions that erupt in the moment like the mom with her child, or they may be a continual process of experiencing the other through the lens of unfinished business like the man feeling neglected by his spouse. We are all wounded. That is, we all have had traumatic experiences that we have not fully processed. Our experiences of others and our reactions to others are significantly affected by these wounds. Although we would ultimately choose to be kind, loving, and giving, we cannot help but act, at times, in ways that are unkind and hurtful.

Earlier, I claimed, "Our level of choice is a function of our level of consciousness." Reacting out of our unfinished business is an example of unconsciousness. We are experiencing the effect of our unfinished business without awareness. On the other hand, consciousness involves being aware that our "stuff" was triggered, allowing us to deal with that instead of blaming the other. Consciousness creates a moment of choice that allows us to avoid acting in unkind and hurtful ways. Consciousness for the mom (discussed above) would involve an awareness of her anger and being present with it. Once the anger subsides, she can address the issue with her child from a centered place, one that is loving, even if she feels the need to impose a consequence for the child's behavior. Consciousness separates the triggered emotion, usually grounded in unfinished business, from our interaction with the other. Our emotion is a result of what has been activated in us. It is not really about the other. We cannot really see and relate lovingly to the other without first dealing with the emotion that has been triggered. Unfortunately, most of us react unconsciously a good deal of the time.

There are two important implications of this observation. First, when people act in unkind or hurtful ways toward us, they are not against us. They are acting out of their own unconsciousness. They are reacting out of their own unfinished business. Further, they may be seeing us as for or against *them*. Second, much of what we take to be unkind, inconsiderate, or insensitive is a product of our own unconsciousness. That is, we are seeing what the other did through our own unfinished business. To an objective observer, it might not be unkind or even noteworthy. Nobody is against us. People are just being themselves in their own limited ways.

One benefit of realizing that no one is against us is avoiding or letting go of grudges. How many people have their energy tied up in what someone did to them in the past? Holding a grudge harms the person holding it, not the one it targets. If we realize that they were just being themselves, acting out of their own unconsciousness, *and* we likely experienced what they did through our own unconsciousness, there is no reason to blame them. What they did was not about us. Note that this is *not* forgiveness. Forgiveness is a belief that they did something to us (against us), but we are willing to stop blaming. What we are discussing goes further. It frees us from the story that they did something to us and from the need to blame them at all.

A caveat is important here. This is not a claim that whatever people do is acceptable or that they are not responsible for their behaviors. Rather, we have the opportunity to recognize that we do not need to take their actions as personal. Further, we can be aware that our reactions and perceptions of their actions are skewed by our unfinished business.

27

But what about our sense that people are *for* us? Certainly, that is more pleasant and creates less conflict. But let's raise some questions about that too. Consider the following two examples. A couple has fallen in love. They have a strong sense that the other is *for them*. They decide to move in together. After some period of time, they start to have conflicts; they are disappointed, feel hurt, experience less love. What happened? Initially, to earn the other's love, each was focused on giving the other what the other wanted. Once they were living together, they went back to their normal way of interacting–wanting and expecting from the other. The partner was not previously for them any more than they are now against them.

A person begins seeing a therapist. He is extremely pleased with the relationship he is developing with the therapist. The therapist is accepting, loving, kind, and attentive. The therapist seems to be clearly *for him*. After a few months, the therapist suggests that he come to group therapy. He agrees to try it. In the group, it becomes clear that the therapist treats everyone in an accepting, loving, kind, attentive manner. Was the therapist really for him? What he initially interpreted as *for him* is a characteristic of the therapist and not personal at all.

So maybe no one is actually for us or against us. There is a freedom in this acknowledgement. If we realize that it is our unfinished business, our unconsciousness that leads us to experience others as being for us or against us, we can deal with the root of the problem, our unfinished business. We can deal with it by completing and releasing our triggered emotions. Completing our unfinished business opens the possibility of seeing others as they are and accepting them as loving at times but struggling with their own unfinished business at other times. We don't have to take their behaviors personally. We can love them as they are, not conditional on how they fit our expectations.

This leaves one crucial question, "How do we complete and release our unfinished business?" This is the central theme of Chapter 7, "Dealing with Uncomfortable Emotions."

CHAPTER 6

Fear

In our lives we experience both pain and suffering. Although they are related, understanding the difference between the two is important. Pain is a natural aspect of being alive. Physical pain is natural, serving as a critical signal of injury and illness. Emotional pain is also natural. Suffering, on the other hand, is not a necessary condition of being alive, yet almost everyone experiences it. Let's take a couple of examples. When we get an injection in a doctor's office, we are likely to feel pain very briefly. However, some people, when they know they have to get an injection, are stressed, anxious, and maybe even physically ill for several days before. That's suffering. If somebody we love dies or leaves us, we experience emotional pain. That is a natural human response. However, if someone loses a loved one, and five years later, they are still miserable and shut down, that is suffering. An important part of spirituality is learning how to avoid or minimize suffering. (Chapter 11 provides a detailed discussion of this distinction.) In this chapter, we discuss one of the greatest sources of suffering, fear.

Fear is an evolutionary gift that we share with many different types of animals. It is a gift because it contributes to survival. When an animal sees, hears, or smells a nearby predator, the fear response energizes its fight-or-flight response perhaps saving it from the predator. We humans also have this response to a physical threat. However, we experience fear regularly even though we are rarely physically threatened. What is the source of this fear?

Three elements combine to create our experience of fear: a trigger, an anticipated experience, and an expectation of a negative impact from the experience. Let's take an example. Marie meets the new person in her spouse's office. The new person is very attractive. Marie fears that her spouse will get involved with the new person and that, as a result, she will be devastated. The trigger was meeting the new person. The anticipated experience was an affair between Marie's spouse and the new person. The expectation of negative impact was Marie's devastation resulting from the affair. All three are necessary. If Marie had not believed that her spouse could get involved with this person, there would have been no fear. If she believed in the potential affair but had not expected it to devastate her (e.g., she had been looking for a way out of the marriage), there would have been no fear. Triggers of fear are only triggers if they are combined with the other two elements. We will return to these elements when we discuss dealing with fear.

First, let's discuss why we experience fear when there is no physical threat. Such fear is the product of the ego mind. The ego mind is always trying to establish a measure of control in our lives. Specifically, it wants to get or keep what makes us okay and avoid that which disturbs us. The ego mind often cannot prevent disturbances, but it believes that anticipating them gives it some level of control. Some people actually verbalize this belief. "I want to know if there is an attractive new person at my spouse's work, so if they get involved, it doesn't take me by surprise." But does fearing an event

31

give us some control over the impact of that event should it occur? Before we address this question, let's make a distinction.

The distinction is between fear and rational precaution. Of course, we buy automobile insurance, fasten our seat belts, have regular medical, dental, and vision exams. But we don't do these things out of fear. We do these things because they are reasonable ways to maintain our health and possessions. Fear is an experience of stress that may or may not lead to some kind of action.

How many things are there to be afraid of? The things we fear are only a miniscule percentage of the negative events that could occur. Recognizing this fact makes the ego mind's attempts at control seem ludicrous. Some of us fear some things more intensely than others. Some of us have more fears than others. But we are all dealing with fear. There is no shortage of triggers. When we see someone suffering from physical or mental illness or disability, it can trigger fear of it happening to us. When a friend or loved one goes through a difficult time, it can trigger fear in us. News reports, stories we read or hear can serve as triggers. Alas, we don't need external triggers, our minds are fully capable of triggering fear, both when we are awake and when we are dreaming.

There are two outcomes with respect to what we fear. The vast majority of what we fear will never happen. A tiny percentage of what we fear will happen. Consider the following example. Yuki's mother died of breast cancer when Yuki was 40 years old. At 80 years of age, Yuki dies in her sleep of natural causes. Although she never developed breast cancer, a tragedy ensued anyway. For forty years, half of her life, Yuki suffered from the fear that she would get breast cancer, something that never happened. How many of us are creating suffering related to multiple possible occurrences?

Now consider the case of Yuki again. This time the story is different. At age 69, Yuki is diagnosed with breast cancer. Yuki suffered from her fear for almost three decades while healthy and now she is ill. Getting back to our earlier question, Is Yuki better off having feared breast cancer all of these years? Has that given her more control over the situation?

One of the ways that people deal with fear is to arm themselves against what they are afraid of. Let's consider a couple of cases. First, let's return to the case of Yuki. Yuki's doctor recommended that she get a mammogram every year beginning at age 40. However, because of her fear, Yuki goes for a mammogram three times a year. Perhaps it is wise for her to get more than one mammogram a year. But the question is, how does getting three mammograms a year affect her fear? The extra mammograms do nothing to alleviate the fear. In fact, for several weeks before each mammogram, Yuki's fear intensifies as she awaits the test and its results.

Now consider Edgar, who works for a company. Edgar is afraid that his boss does not like him, and if she does not, he will not be promoted and might even be fired. Edgar responds to his fear by constantly trying to get on the good side of his boss. He praises her, offers to do extra tasks for her, and laughs at her jokes. Is it wise to maintain a good relationship with one's boss? Sure. But what is happening to Edgar's fear? It is not decreasing. The constant acting from fear reinforces it and probably makes it stronger. He second-guesses his efforts, which also increases his fear. What both of these examples show us is that acting out of fear, trying to make sure what we fear does not happen, does not decrease our fear and likely increases it.

So, how can we deal with fear in a constructive way? I offer three principles for doing so. First, we cannot use the mind to get rid of fear. The mind has created the stories about the future that are the source of our fears (the predicted occurrences and the expectations of negative impact). These stories are not real, because they are not what is happening. But the mind considers them to be real. Asking the mind to be the solution to fear is asking the fox to guard the henhouse.

The second principle is that we cannot get rid of fear by focusing on the content of our fears, what we are afraid of. Why? Because, as we discussed, there are an unlimited number of things that we can fear, so it is impossible to deal with each one.

Finally, the third principle follows from the first two. We must deal with fear, and not the content of our fears, in a way that does not depend on the mind. We will refer to this process as "releasing fear." In Chapter 7, "Dealing with Uncomfortable Emotions," we will explore a way to release all uncomfortable emotions including fear.

Q1. Are fear and worry related?

A1. For the purposes of this discussion, worry may be considered a less intense manifestation of fear. Worry is a product of the mind and involves a trigger, an expected occurrence, and an expectation of negative impact from that occurrence. It may be easier to work initially with worries and build up to tackling larger fears.

Q2. What about anxiety?

A2. Although we use "anxiety" colloquially, it is a clinical diagnosis. Severe anxiety should be treated by an expert. Moderate anxiety, which may not have a clear trigger, expected occurrence, or expectation of negative impact, may also be released through the process described in Chapter 7.

CHAPTER 7

Dealing with Uncomfortable Emotions

I n this chapter, I share the spiritual practice that has had the greatest impact on my life.

Emotions are meant to come up, be experienced fully, and pass. When the emotion that arises is one that we like, we generally are willing to experiencing it fully–but not always. Some of us are afraid to feel certain positive emotions because we fear that they will open us up to subsequent negative emotions. For example, a person may be afraid to really feel love in a relationship because of the fear of being hurt if the relationship ends. But for most of us the real challenge is fully experiencing emotions that are painful or uncomfortable. As we discussed in a prior chapter, experiencing painful emotions is a natural part of being human. However, suffering is created by our *response* to painful emotions.

Let's examine the impact of different ways people deal with painful or uncomfortable emotions beginning with more extreme examples and then moving to more common ones. Emily's husband died suddenly five years ago. She has been an emotional wreck ever since (her own assessment). She still has regular crying jags. All kinds of experiences trigger emotions related to her husband's death. She still cannot bear to enter their shared bedroom and is unable to lead a "normal life." Emily's painful emotions caused by losing her husband are natural. However, her inability to function normally years later is an example of suffering.

Fernando's wife left him five years ago. Fernando has been unable to have a serious relationship since then and is unable to feel much for anyone. People who know him observe that his affect is very flat. Fernando is committed to not getting hurt like that again. He has dealt with his painful emotions by closing his heart. He is suffering as well. One thing that Fernando and Emily have in common is that they seem to have less energy than they did five years ago.

The examples of Emily and Fernando are reactions to painful emotions. If you have not had a similar experience, you probably know someone who has. But let's turn now to more commonplace examples. James is sitting and watching television. His wife comes in and says, "I thought you were going to take out the garbage." James says angrily, "I'll do it. Get off my back!" In a second example, it is Jasmine's birthday. By evening, Jasmine's daughter has not called to wish her a happy birthday. Jasmine is distraught. Finally, Belle and her wife Sara are going out for dinner. Belle puts on a new blouse that she bought for the occasion. She says to Sara, "Do you like this blouse?" Sara responds, "It's alright." Belle is so hurt she cannot enjoy her dinner.

What do these three examples have in common? First, we have all had experiences like these. We have likely been both the one reacting and the one being reacted to. Second, in each case, the reaction seems disproportionate to the trigger. A minor event was met with a strong reaction. Let's explore what is behind these three examples, and the two more extreme ones.

As I said in the opening to this chapter, "Emotions are meant to come up, be experienced fully, and pass." However, what happens when we do not experience the emotion fully? In that case we are left with unfinished business. The uncomfortable emotion has not been completed and passed. This results in what has been termed an "energy block," an image that I find helpful in discussing the impact of emotions that have not been fully processed. An energy block has three attributes. First, it is like a large rock that has been placed in a stream, partially impeding the normal flow, in the case of an energy block, the flow of our energy (sometimes called "life force", "qi", "shakti", or "prana"). This is related to the second attribute. In creating an energy block, we tie up a certain amount of our energy. It takes continued energy to avoid feeling the emotion, to hold the unfinished emotion away from our awareness. The third attribute is that, as long as the block is there, the emotion at its core can be reignited, triggered by life events or even thoughts.

Let's discuss further this third attribute. Although energy blocks inevitably get triggered, there is no entity that is *trying* to trigger them. By analogy, imagine that you have a sore finger. Life inevitably hits that finger. Someone squeezes your hand. You hit your finger getting dressed. You pick up something with that hand. The fact that it is sore makes it vulnerable to normal life events. This is also the case for an energy block. If you have energy blocks, life will hit them. Let's take an example.

Paul calls from work and says to his spouse, "I just found out that my old friend, Robin is in town for just this evening, so we are going to dinner. I will see you if you are still up when I get home.

38

Paul's spouse gets very sullen on the phone and has a big reaction upon hanging up. Thoughts come such as, "He used to be excited to come home to me. Maybe he is bored with me or wants to leave me." Bernie makes an identical call. His spouse responds, "Oh, how nice! Have a great time." What is the difference? Paul's spouse had an energy block triggered by the phone call. When the block got hit strong emotions that had not been fully processed in the past were triggered. If those strong emotions are not fully experienced this time, the energy block will become even larger. The next time it is hit, the reaction is likely to be even greater. On the other hand, Bernie's spouse had no block triggered by the call, so his spouse was able to respond in a loving manner. We all have energy blocks. However, each person's set of blocks are unique, so we may be triggered by different events. What we begin to see from this example is that our emotional reactions are not *caused* by whomever or whatever triggered the reaction. Rather, the block getting hit causes our reaction. If there is nothing to get hit, there is little or no reaction. As we discussed, if a block exists, it will get hit. Thus, it is more effective to get rid of the block than to try to prevent the block from getting hit.

Before we talk about how to get rid of energy blocks, let's consider the ways that people respond to uncomfortable emotions. Most of us know only two ways, *suppressing* or *expressing* the emotion. Suppressing involves being in denial about the emotion. We might talk ourselves out of it, "It's really no big deal; there is nothing to be angry about." We might just ignore what is happening inside us, stuffing the emotion. We might distract ourselves with work or entertainment. We might "medicate" using alcohol, food, or drugs. Each of these approaches is an attempt to not feel the emotion. These approaches seem to work in the moment and are considered normal, but they only increase the energy block. The next time the block gets triggered the reaction might be harder to control.

While we are talking about suppressing emotions, let's consider an encouragement to suppress that we often hear from our friends and family. Losing a loved one can trigger some of the most painful emotions. Soon after such an event, we receive the well-intended advice, "Keep busy." "Immerse yourself in work." "Distract yourself so you don't think about ___ [name of loved one]." These are culturally approved approaches to suppressing emotions.

Expressing an emotion is also a typical response to uncomfortable emotions. We might yell when we feel angry or pound our fist when we feel frustration. The feeling of wanting to scream or hit something is common when we feel strong reactions. Expressing emotions often creates problems when we aim our expressing at the person who triggered the emotion. Whereas these actions are a way to dump the energy in the moment, they do nothing to remove the block that has been hit. In fact, the block is likely to grow. For example, we might find that our explosions of anger get more frequent and more intense.

The good news is that there is a third way to respond to uncomfortable emotions. Rather than suppress or express, we can *release* these emotions. Releasing emotions reduces energy blocks instead of creating or growing them. Releasing an emotion involves consciously experiencing an emotion completely. Once experienced, the emotion passes. The result is no unfinished business and therefore no new energy blocks. But, as we discussed, in adulthood, most of our emotional responses are a result of a triggering event hitting an already established energy block. In this scenario, by consciously experiencing the emotion, the disturbed energy hits the energy block unimpeded resulting in the diminishment or elimination of the block. For example, if one typically has explosive angry reactions, releasing these reactions results in these reactions becoming weaker and perhaps less frequent. This diminishment of our energy blocks through releasing emotions is a natural healing process. Just as healing of the body (e.g., healing of a cut on the arm) takes place naturally if we do not interfere with it, dissolution of energy blocks happens naturally if we allow it to.

When an uncomfortable emotion is triggered, we emerge from the experience either more open or more closed. If we suppress or express the emotion, we become more closed. We tie up more of our energy to avoid feeling the unfinished emotion. If we release the emotion, we dissolve part or all of the energy block that was hit. Energy that was tied up is released, and, as a result, we are more open. I experienced this in stark contrast. I had two romantic relationships end similarly one before I knew about releasing and one just after I learned about releasing. After the first breakup, I struggled for a long time. However, after the second breakup, I endured a short painful period in which I diligently committed to releasing. The result was a quicker recovery, some powerful energetic experiences, and a surprising result. A few friends and colleagues came up to me and said that they experienced me as "softer" and "more open." In fact, I could feel that my heart was more open. I was able to be more vulnerable rather than less. I had less reason to protect myself as I had less of a block to defend.

So how do we release emotions? Here I describe the process that I learned initially from a Mickey Singer audio recording and the modifications that have come from my own practice. Note that I am not claiming that this is the only way to release emotions. Merely it is a way that has been powerful for me. The instructions are as follows.

When you are first aware of an uncomfortable emotion (large or small), sit up straight or lie on your back, open your chest, relax your body, and focus on (observe) the feeling in your body. You might feel a churning in your belly, a pain in your heart, or a tightening in your shoulders or jaw. The feeling might change, intensify, or lessen. Whatever you feel, observe it and do nothing about it. This is the energy doing its work. Watch the feelings in your body until the acute feelings subside. You do not need to label the emotion, and you do not need to know anything about the origin of the energy block that has been activated. If your mind starts talking about the trigger (e.g., "How dare she talk to me that way?") or distracting you, just let it go and return to the sensations in your body. That is the basic practice. For strong emotions, you may notice that opening the chest is the opposite of what you are inclined to do. In these situations, most of us want to curl up in the fetal position protecting the heart. Opening the chest represents physically opening to the energy that has been activated and letting it do its work.

The main modification that I have made to the practice is to consciously express my gratitude for the experience. Of course, no one volunteers for painful emotions. However, once in the situation and knowing that it is an opportunity for healing, for dissolution of my energy blocks, I can honestly express gratitude for the opportunity to engage in this process. I also often express my desire to receive the full intensity, knowing that the stronger the energy, the more work it can do. Ultimately, I want the greatest possible dissolution of the block that has been hit.

So why have I added an expression of gratitude to my practice? I have found that, unintentionally, I may engage in subtle resistance to the uncomfortable feeling created by the emotion. Although I am attempting to open completely to the experience of the emotion, my tendency to protect myself might still be active at some level. I find that if I can sincerely welcome and be grateful for the experience, I cannot resist at the same time. My gratitude supports my openness.

At this point, I offer a physical analogy for the releasing process. Most of us, at some time in our lives, have had a deep massage. If you have a knot (a tight muscle), perhaps in your back or your neck, you want the massage therapist to push on the knot and try to work it out–knowing that it is likely to be painful. The therapist begins to push on the knot. If you tighten up and try to protect yourself from the pain or the expected pain, you will not benefit from the massage and might even increase the tension in that area. You will keep and maybe grow the knot. If, on the other hand, you relax and open, allowing the therapist to work on the block, even if painful, the block will likely be diminished. In fact, most of us who value deep massage tend to say when the therapist hits the block, "Yes, right there." We encourage the therapist to push harder and stay in that spot longer. We do this with an understanding that the more aggressive work may result in greater benefit. This corresponds to what I said about releasing emotions, I also often express the desire to receive the full intensity, knowing that the stronger the energy, the more work it can do.

When people first engage in this practice, there is one trap that they often fall into. The trap can be characterized by the following internal complaint. "I've been observing the feeling in my body for thirty seconds and it still hasn't gone away." This represents a fundamental misunderstanding. This practice is not something you *do* to get rid of the uncomfortable feeling. Trying to get rid of it is a type of resistance. Releasing emotions involves being present and permitting the process to take place. As we said, it is a natural healing process. Let's consider the analogy of healing the physical body. Imagine someone has a cut on the arm and says, "I have been conscious not to injure it further and to keep it clean. It has been two days, and I still have a scab." You would likely respond by saying that the healing process needs to be given the time it needs. There is nothing one can do to speed it up. The same is true with releasing emotions.

One of the impacts of witnessing the physical effects of an emotion is that it helps us let go of our attention to the trigger (blame). When we focus on what is happening in the body, we are witnessing an *internal* process, and our story about the *external* trigger (the cause of the emotion) fades into the background. Of course, the ego mind may distract us with its story about the trigger. When we notice it, we return our focus to what is manifesting in the body.

Some people with whom I share this practice respond in a way that suggests they don't see the difference between what they are already doing and the practice that we have been discussing. This invites a subtle but important distinction. Let's take an example. In response to learning about this process, Naomi says, "My wife died three months ago. I am *aware* that I am grieving, that I am sad; I cry a lot. So, how is this practice different?" Naomi, like most people who have not learned about releasing emotions, is immersed in her grief. She is identified with her grief. It is her nature at this time. This is different from the practice that we have been discussing. The practice involves witnessing the emotion. The emotion comes and, if fully experienced, passes. Witnessing the emotion allows us to know ourselves as the consciousness, the awareness. We are not the emotion. The emotion is the object of our consciousness. Let me share my personal experience of the distinction invited by Naomi's question.

When I have undergone an emotionally painful event, such as losing a loved one, this distinction has become clear. If I try to go on with my life normally (e.g., get some work done, watch television), my grief seems to hover over me. It is like being under a dark cloud. I suffer. I am not okay. However, if I engage in the process of releasing the emotion, the pain may be the same of even more intense, but I do not suffer. I am okay. I am the one watching the pain and welcoming the energy that has been triggered. I am participating in a therapeutic process, not suffering from an ongoing, bleak experience. The pain is of limited duration and beneficial. Before I knew about the process of releasing, I would have said that my grief was and would be present every waking hour for a considerable period. However, as I have practiced releasing, I have become aware that grief comes and goes, and if I stop and engage in releasing each time it comes, I feel pain, but I do not suffer. What is more, I am benefitting from the process. It leaves me more open and less obstructed by my energy blocks.

There is a corollary to this practice that I have learned through experience. I introduce this corollary by returning to the example of Emily, whose husband died suddenly. Over the next weeks and months, there are things that she is avoiding doing, because, in her words, "It makes it real." "It has been many months, but I don't want to go through my husband's stuff, because it will be too painful. I don't even sleep in our bedroom. I have been avoiding dealing with the life insurance, because it seems so final." Of course, there is nothing wrong with the choices that Emily is making, and indeed many people would make the same choices. However, the corollary to the practice we have been discussing involves very different choices.

The corollary is based on the following realization. If I have something in me that can be triggered, it will be triggered. Therefore, I want it to be triggered and removed; I do not want to preserve it. In the case of a triggering event that has occurred, it means taking full advantage of it. It means moving *towards* related triggering elements rather than away from them. Each of the potentially triggering elements that Emily is avoiding (her husband's clothes, the shared bedroom, his life insurance) could be used to trigger and release. If we are sincerely committed to eliminating our blocks, we don't avoid triggers, we use them. This is true not only for major events like losing a loved one, but also for less significant events. For example, you had an uncomfortable interaction with a neighbor. You typically walk past his house on the way to the supermarket. Do you walk your normal route, or do you find a way to walk so as not to run into him?

One clarification on the example in the last paragraph. I am not advocating that Emily go through her husband's things in the first weeks after his death. The discussion is not about timing. Rather, the discussion highlights a difference between seeing that event as something to be avoided as long as possible versus seeing it as an event with healing potential.

Note that releasing emotions is an internal process. After doing so, the situation that triggered the emotion might still require some attention. For example, there might be a conversation needed with the loved one or colleague who triggered the emotion. Being in a centered, fully present state rather than a reactive one allows us to have a more constructive, more self-responsible, and more loving conversation.

There is a wonderful additional benefit from regularly engaging in releasing uncomfortable emotions. We become less afraid of our emotions. Are we afraid of our emotions? Every event we fear, we fear *because* we are afraid of how it will make us feel. The more experience we have releasing uncomfortable emotions, particularly painful emotions, the more we know that we will be okay regardless of what emotions are triggered. How liberating would that be? We would no longer need to live in fear and organize our lives around avoiding situations that might cause painful emotions.

I have described a way of dealing with uncomfortable emotions, a way that is not suppressing and is not expressing. I have shared some of the powerful benefits that I have experienced from it. However, like everything else in this book, you should not take my word for it. Is this an experiment worth doing?

CHAPTER 8

Is the Mind a Problem?

In many spiritual teachings and writings, the mind gets a bad rap. We frequently hear about the "monkey mind," quieting the mind, and getting out of the mind. The mind is often characterized as the source of our problems. Is the mind a problem? Let's delve a little deeper into the role of the mind in our lives.

The most significant point one can make about the mind is that most of us identify with it. We believe that we are the mind. But are we the mind? First of all, let's consider the mind's content. You may have noticed that most of the mind's content arises uninvited. You are trying NOT to think about what is happening tomorrow, but it keeps popping up. A song gets stuck in your head, and you'd love to get it out. You are doing one thing and distracting thoughts come into your head. Is all of that content who we are? No, we are the one who is aware of what is going on in our mind. We are the observer of the mind's content. We are no more the mind than we are the television show we are watching. We are the consciousness. The content of the mind is the object of consciousness. However, we have grown up and spent most of our lives identified with the mind.

So, is the mind a problem or a gift? It is indeed a gift. The human mind is a tremendous tool. It has been used for incredible achievements and inventions in various fields including engineering, mathematics, and science. So how did the mind get its bad rap? It got its bad rap through misuse. Any tool can be misused. For example, suppose you use a high-quality, well-maintained knife to pry open a can or turn a screw. The blade breaks and you are injured. The problem is not the knife. Rather, the knife was used for a purpose it was not designed for. That is the story of the human mind.

Let's examine the tool–the mind–and then discuss its misuse. The power of the mind comes from its ability to *learn*. For our purpose here, I will only consider one type of learning. People have all kinds of experiences. Some seem to have no effect on their well-being. Notice all the things you see, hear, and smell in a day that have no impact on you and, as a result, are not memorable. However, some of our experiences have either a positive or negative effect on us physically or emotionally. The mind stores these in memory along with a designation. This designation of the positive or negative effect indicates whether the experience, or a similar experience, should be sought or avoided, desired or feared. This seems normal and appropriate. So where does the problem arise?

The problem comes from our identification with the ego mind. One key feature of this identification is that it gives the ego mind responsibility for our being okay. The mind is fully capable of giving us good advice about ways to be okay physically: have annual checkups, eat healthfully, exercise regularly, wear seatbelts and sunscreen, etc. However, we have given the ego mind responsibility for making us okay inside. But what does it know about being okay inside? It only knows what it has "learned." And it has learned in the only way it can. It has sorted past experiences into how they made us feel–whether they made us feel more or less okay?

49

And what does the mind do with these "learnings?" It tells us that we will be okay *in the future* if we get more of what we want or desire and less of what we do not want or fear. We are in constant pursuit of everything the mind tells us we need: a nice house, a new car, a partner, a child, a grandchild, more recognition, more money, or for our loved ones to act in certain ways. Simultaneously, we're driven by the fear of what we need to avoid: injury, illness, degenerative problems, loss of loved ones, public humiliation, and financial loss. We are continually busy and stressed as we pursue what we want and avoid what we don't want. We are in conflict with how life is showing up and fearful of how it might show up. We are constantly postponing being okay in favor of the promise of being so in the future. We are focused on getting and avoiding things outside in an effort to make the inside okay. This is a strategy that cannot work.

In addition to this unfulfilling pursuit of the ego mind's agenda, the ego mind prevents us from perceiving life as it is. We are continually seeing each experience in terms of how it resembles prior experiences that the mind has labeled as positive or negative, and thus in terms of how it fits with the ego mind's agenda. By analogy, there is a reason we do not want sports referees who are rooting for one of the teams. People who want particular outcomes tend to see what happens in ways that fit with their interests. We see our interactions with others according to how they fit with what we want and do not want, not as they are.

The problem is not having a mind. As we've discussed, the mind is a great tool that can be used to accomplish great things. The problem is that **we have given the mind a responsibility it is not equipped for—making us okay.** We are misusing this great tool. The mind has no access to the source of peace, love, joy, and equanimity. In fact, by giving the mind the responsibility for our well-being, it puts us on a path AWAY from those very qualities. Why? Because these qualities can only be found in the present, and the ego mind cannot exist in the present. The ego mind is engaged in creating a future based on the past. It is focused on what we need to be okay—what we need to get and avoid in the outside world.

So, the problem is not that we have a mind. The problem is our identification with the mind, giving the mind the responsibility for our being okay. The ego mind will continue to give us bad advice. This is only a problem if we accept that advice and live according to it. When we turn on the television, we are bombarded with bad advice: drink soda, eat fast food, take drugs for everything that ails us. We learn to ignore that advice, and we can learn to ignore the advice from our ego minds. When the ego mind says, "I (notice it uses the first person) will be happy when I get a promotion and make more money," or "I will be happy when I find a romantic partner who is more attractive and more exciting," we can ignore this advice. We do not have to fight with the mind or seek to improve it. We just need to recognize that the ego mind is not who we are and let its unhelpful advice pass.

CHAPTER 9

Intimate Relationships

Humans tend to seek relationships. The question is, why? Generally, we seek relationships because of what we believe they will bring us, such as acceptance, love, respect, and security. We seek relationships to make us feel less alone and to feel valued.

It is important to realize that we pursue these qualities in relationships because we feel a lack of these qualities within ourselves. We seek acceptance because we are self-rejecting. We seek love because we feel unsure of our lovability. We seek security because we are afraid. We seek companionship because we feel lonely. We question our value and seek to have others reflect our value back to us. However, when we attempt to get what we are lacking through our relationships, it prevents us from forming *real* relationships.

We do not have genuine relationships because we fail to see, experience, and know the other person. Let's explore this point first in contexts that do not involve relationships with other humans. If we go outside in the evening to watch the sunset, we see the sunset as it is. If we hear a new piece of music, we generally hear it as it is. We experience these events as they are because we have "nothing going" with them.

On the other hand, imagine you are entering a house and are afraid someone dangerous is inside. Do you experience the house as it is? No, your focus is on the places where someone might be hiding. As a result, you do not see much of what is there. Imagine now that you enter the same house hoping that someone you love and have not seen for a long time is somewhere in the house. Do you experience the house as it is? These scenarios highlight something we know at some level but are not cognizant of; when we have no want or desire, no fear or avoidance, we can experience what is *as it is*. But when we come to a situation with want, desire, fear, or avoidance, we do not experience the situation as it is; we see only select aspects in terms of how they fit into what we want and do not want.

This applies to relationships with people as well. We are unable to experience the people we are in relationship with *as they are* because of the wants, desires, fears, and avoidances we bring to those relationships. *We see others in terms of how they meet or fail to meet our expectations.* If we are looking for love, we are attentive to whether their actions are loving or unloving (as *we* perceive them). If we are looking for acceptance, we are focused on the acceptance we feel or do not feel from them. We cannot really know them, because we are busy sorting their behaviors and attributes according to how they align with what we want and do not want.

We not only assess what we are getting from the other, but we try to influence them. Through our words and actions, we try to encourage them to act more in ways that we want and to discourage them from acting in ways we do not want. If after some period of trying, we are getting too little of what we want or too much of what we do not want, we may go looking for another partner who will do better. This is one of the main reasons people get into extra-marital

53

relationships. The relationship with the new person seems to hold the promise of giving us what we are looking for, in contrast with our partner, who has failed to deliver over time.

You might respond, "But surely it is appropriate to have some expectations: honesty, monogamy, communication, sex, sharing of responsibilities." This response invites an important distinction. Expectations about such basic tenets of the relationship are not a problem. The inability to see the other derives from expectations about how the other should make us feel. "I should no longer feel lonely, insecure, afraid, or bored. I should feel valued, confident, and competent." When we enter into a relationship expecting that our fears and insecurities will disappear or be greatly diminished, we are ripe for disappointment. No one can do this for us.

But what about love? We love feeling great love, but how often do we feel it and for how long? Consider the following. You are having breakfast with your partner. You are feeling love for your partner. Just then, your partner complains about the chores that you have neglected in favor of your golf outings. What happens to the love you were feeling? It seems to have disappeared in an instant. If we are honest with ourselves this phenomenon happens regularly.

Consider a second example. You have been single for a while, and just recently, you met someone and fell in love. You suddenly feel more love for your friends, family, and colleagues. You even feel love for people you encounter in stores and at the gym. What can we glean from these examples?

First, your partner in the first example and the people you encounter in the second example did not cause the love you were feeling. The love comes from within. The second example helps us see that the flow of love happens when our hearts are open, the more open our hearts are, the more love flows. (See Chapter 4, "The Open Heart.") However, the first example also shows us what happens to that flow of love when we close our hearts. It is like a water hose. Water pours out of it, but if it is crimped, the flow slows down and can even stop completely. So, if love comes from and through us, it is not the responsibility of our partners to make us feel love. If we are not feeling great love for our partner, it is not that we are with the wrong partner. Rather, it is we are failing to open our hearts and to keep our hearts open.

Our partners are not responsible for how we feel. Being in a relationship will not make our internal experience what we want it to be. Perhaps, everything seems perfect at the outset, but it cannot last. Each partner will eventually settle into trying to get what they want. Each will fail to see the other as they are. Changing partners does not change this truth. So, what can we do?

We can take responsibility for what is not okay in us. It is not our partner's responsibility to fix it. We can let go of expectations of our partner when they come up. We can work to open our hearts and to reopen our hearts when they close. As we let go of our expectations and open our hearts, we can see and accept our partners as they are. Perhaps then we can have a *real* relationship with our partner.

Q1. In this more spiritual relationship that you are describing, where does personal sharing and vulnerability come into play?

A1. Sharing and vulnerability are important aspects of being in an intimate relationship. They allow the other person to know and see us. Our communication no longer focuses on our expectations and our emotional responses to those expectations not being met. Rather, we take responsibility for our reactions and expectations and communicate about the work we are doing to let go of them. In doing so, the other may simply listen to our process or engage in some work of their own. The intimacy of a relationship is enhanced by openness and acceptance (of ourselves and of the other).

Q2. If we are taking responsibility for our reactions and expectations, are there still situations in which we might choose to leave the relationship?

A2. This is an important question. Most people end relationships either because they are unable to complete and release their reactions to the other person or because the other person is not making them feel the way they want to feel. However, if we are doing the work to let go of both our reactions and our expectations, we are better able to see the other and the relationship as they are. When we are seeing clearly, we can make choices about continuing or ending the relationship. Such choices are made with love, not out of anger, hurt, or disappointment. They are not made under the illusion that finding the "right" partner will make us feel the way we want to feel.

CHAPTER 10

We Have Only One Problem

W*e have only one problem*. Really? Most of us could list a plethora of problems in multiple areas of our lives: physical problems, work problems, family problems, and social problems. Where do all these problems come from? They are the creation of the ego mind. You might be thinking, "No, my problems are real." They *are* real—for the ego mind.

The ego mind attempts to take care of us, to make us okay. It does so in the only way it can. It uses its memories of the past to determine what in the future will make us okay and what will make us not okay. As a result, it tries to manage our lives so we have the experiences that will make us okay and avoid those that will make us not okay. However, this agenda *creates* problems.

Everything that we need or want, and everything that we fear or do not want becomes a problem when life does not conform to our wants. Each instance in which we are in conflict with reality is a problem. If I have a problem with my hip, and my mind says, "In order to be okay, I need to be pain-free and have no restriction," then I have a problem. If my mind says, "I need to have a child or a grandchild," and having a child or grandchild does not seem to be on the horizon, I have a problem. If my mind says, "I need to get promoted at work," and no promotion is forthcoming, I have a problem. The important thing is not what the problem is, but where the problem comes from. The problem comes from the ego mind deciding what we need and what we must avoid. The only thing we can be sure of is that life will not conform to what the ego mind is dictating. Why should it? Reality unfolds independent of what our minds say about it.

We have established so far that inevitably the ego mind has many problems. However, I said at the outset that we have only *one* problem. What is that problem? The problem is that we don't know who we are. We have mistakenly identified ourselves with the ego mind. This misidentification puts the ego mind in charge. That is our *only* problem. Let's examine what happens if we resolve this problem.

If we begin to witness the ego mind, its constant activity, its dictates about what we need and must avoid, we realize that we are not the ego mind. Rather we are the one who is aware of it–the consciousness. Knowing ourselves as the consciousness and not the ego mind frees us from accepting the dictates of the ego mind as reality.

So, what might life be like if we were to know ourselves as the consciousness? Consider the analogy of sitting on the couch watching a movie. We are absolutely fine and enjoying the movie, regardless of the content. It can be funny, sad, or thrilling. The main characters can have success or failure; they can live or die. We are okay because we are the one watching the movie. Life is like that. If we are the consciousness, we can observe changes in our social interactions, our work experiences, and our physical bodies. We are aware as the content of our lives continues to unfold. As the consciousness, as the awareness, we are okay no matter what content we are watching.

So, we are witnessing this grand movie we call life. It's a fascinating movie. There are new experiences all the time. Witnessing this movie, we are inherently okay because we don't need it to be any particular way. We can just be totally entertained, totally fascinated by what shows up. Witnessing life, we have no conflict with it.

Let me give you a simple example of how I am learning this lesson. Recently, we moved to the mountains–ten minutes from one of my favorite ski resorts. This was my opportunity to ski multiple days a week. However, a couple of months into the season, I took a hard fall. Although my injuries were not serious, it was clear that, at best, it would be several weeks before I would be able to ski again. I watched my ego mind begin to get disturbed. It was talking about how this was a disaster. "I am leasing a condo near the ski resort, a significant financial commitment, and I am going to miss a significant chunk of the ski season. I have a great opportunity, and I cannot take advantage of it." My ego mind was telling me that this was a situation in which I would not be okay, but I did not have to listen to it. So, I witnessed the ego mind and let go of this message. And what I found was that I *was* okay. I was okay during the month off the snow. I was okay during the weeks of limited physical activity. The movie had gone in an unexpected direction. The movie now included getting more work done on this book. It included doing exercises and stretches to rehab my injury. Because I was letting go of identification with the ego mind, I was not run by it. By not believing what the ego mind was telling me about what I needed to be okay, I was okay *in the present moment*.

If we do not identify with and listen to the ego mind, we have no problems–just experiences. We can be okay in every moment rather than in conflict with how life shows up. Is that true? Each of us can do this experiment for ourselves.

CHAPTER 11

Pain and Suffering

It is important to understand the difference between *pain* and *suffering*. Let's begin by discussing pain. There are two types of pain: physical pain and emotional pain. Physical pain plays a vital role in our physical well-being. Without it, we would unknowingly harm ourselves, lacking the necessary signals that alert us to bodily issues requiring attention. Not only is physical pain valuable, but it is unavoidable. It is part of the human experience.

As humans, we also experience emotional pain, which can produce painful physical sensations. These sensations, such as heartache, do not indicate physical problems. Emotional pain is also valuable, though its value is less recognized, because most people have not learned to use it constructively. As we discussed in Chapter 7, "Dealing with Uncomfortable Emotions," there are three ways to deal with emotional pain. We can repress, express, or release the emotions. Most people only know about and therefore engage in the first two options. However, it is the third–*release*–that produces positive change. I refer you back to Chapter 7 for a discussion of this process. If we do not know how to use emotional pain, we are unlikely to recognize its value. Emotional pain alerts us to disturbances in our emotions. It too is natural and unavoidable. We all experience grief, fear, anger, embarrassment, and many other painful emotions.

So, pain–whether physical or emotional–is unavoidable. Suffering is not. Suffering is distinct from pain although often related to it. We have the capacity to experience pain without suffering. Let's consider some examples that demonstrate the difference between the two. Imagine going for a vaccination. The prick of the needle can be painful, a natural sensation. However, spending the entire week leading up to it in dread is suffering, an unnecessary addition to the actual pain. One clue that this suffering is not an inherent aspect of the situation is that not everyone experiences pre-injection anxiety.

Consider a romantic relationship that comes to an undesired end. Feeling pain due to the breakup is unavoidable. However, if we remain angry, hurt, and unable to engage in relationships years later, that is suffering.

If we see on the news or read online or in a newspaper about governmental actions that cause us fear, sadness, or anger, this is an instant reaction and a part of being human. However, if such actions cause us to be in a state of depression for months or years at a time, this is suffering–and not required.

Suffering arises from two sources. The first is the failure to consciously engage with a painful experience, preventing the experience from completing and releasing. This is generally more of a concern with emotional pain than with physical pain. The second source of suffering is the expectation that life should conform to our wants and needs. Let's consider these in reverse order.

Most of us have ideas about how life should be, but it seldom conforms to our expectations. For example, we suffer in relationships because our partners do not show up the way we want. They are not nurturing enough, not independent enough, or too independent. They are not interested in some things that we like. They are not ambitious enough, or they are too ambitious. Our ego minds tell us that if our partners were different in particular ways, we would be happier, feel more secure, or feel less alone. This same phenomenon can extend to our bodies, our work life, our families, the economy, and even the weather. We suffer because we want or "need" life to unfold in certain ways. The extent of our suffering is proportional to the discrepancy between our desires and the reality of our circumstances.

We can reduce or eliminate this suffering by letting go of our identification with the ego mind, letting go of its claims about how life needs to be for us to be okay. These messages are seductive. But rather than giving us a path to being okay, they keep us from being okay. They make us suffer when life does not conform to the demands of the ego mind. The alternative is to be present in the adventure, embracing the richness of the current experience, free from conflict with what is.

Take for example someone who accepts his mind's message that his current job is making him unhappy. He may decide to change jobs, and there is nothing wrong with doing so. However, what happens if such a change is not immediate? He dreads going to work each day. He is unhappy while he is at work. He watches the clock, which seems to move incredibly slowly. He is suffering.

Now let's consider the alternative. He lets go of the mind's message, that is he lets go of the belief that his job is making him unhappy. Instead, he goes to work each day ready to experience each moment as it unfolds, each moment as a new adventure. This is often referred to as "beginner's mind," experiencing each moment as it is rather than through the mind's preconceptions about it. This gives him the possibility of finding joy and peace rather than continued conflict. Perhaps, he is also sending out resumes and watching job sites. Being present and okay moment to moment in his job and looking for another job are not in conflict. They are different activities in which he can engage fully at different times.

Injuries, illnesses, conflicts, and losses are inevitable parts of life. We can simply acknowledge our present reality—whether rehabilitating an injury or processing grief. Doing so reframes the experience. Why should rehabbing an injury or processing grief be considered worse than any other activity? What benefit is there in thinking we should be engaged in some other experience, not the one life has brought us? Buying into such thoughts makes us suffer.

Let's now return to the first source of suffering, the inability to release our painful experiences, particularly experiences of emotional pain. We suffer both from the lack of completion of these experiences and from the energy blocks that are created and repeatedly triggered. Consider the following example. A woman is in a romantic relationship. With little warning, her partner announces that the relationship is not working for him and leaves. Of course, this is a painful experience. However, because she does not know how to release the painful experience, suffering ensues. Her uncompleted feeling of abandonment causes her to avoid romantic involvement. Each time there is an opportunity to get close to someone, she creates distance or ends the relationship out of fear of being abandoned again. In addition, the uncompleted feeling has resulted in an energy block that keeps getting triggered. If a friend is late, she panics, feeling that she is being abandoned. If a family member says something that she perceives as critical, she reacts, experiencing this as the beginning of abandonment. But as we discussed, pain is unavoidable, but suffering is not. If we consciously allow the difficult emotions to complete themselves and release (as described in Chapter 7, "Dealing with Uncomfortable Emotions") we eliminate these causes of suffering.

Let's go back to the example of a person suffering in anticipation of receiving a vaccination. It is not the pain of the needle prick that causes the suffering. It may not even be fear of the pain. The fear may be a spontaneous response to anticipation of the vaccination. The suffering comes from not allowing the fear response to fully complete and release.

We have discussed that pain is unavoidable, but suffering is not. If we stand back and look at our lives from this perspective, the pain caused by particular events may have been intense at times, but it generally pales in comparison to the suffering that we induce through our responses to the pain.

CHAPTER 12

Is Life an Illusion?

"What if everything is an illusion...? In that case, I definitely overpaid for my carpet."

Woody Allen, Without Feathers

Sometimes people talk about life as being an illusion. But life is not an illusion, yet we generally live in illusion.

Life exists—it is real—but we do not experience life as it is. Imagine you were wearing glasses with pink lenses, and you did not know you were wearing colored lenses. You would never see life in its true colors; every color would be distorted. This, of course, is just an analogy. In life, the mind is often the distorting lens between "I," the subject, and life.

How does this happen? It happens because of our concepts, desires, fears, and unprocessed emotions. Let's take each of these in turn. Where do our concepts come from? They are learned—they are part of our past. As we've talked about before, the mind learns, it takes an experience and stores a memory of it. The mind forms concepts based on direct experience of someone or something or listening to or reading the concepts of others.

In general, the impact of these concepts is they keep us from seeing what *is* in the moment. They set up expectations. When we encounter a friend, family member, or work colleague, we do not experience them as they are in the moment, but rather we experience them through our thoughts about them. When they behave in certain ways, we interpret their behaviors through our existing concepts of them. If we think someone is manipulative, we're likely to see manipulation in what they do. If we think someone is generous, we're likely to interpret their actions as generous. It becomes very easy for us to start believing that the person actually is who we think they are. But that's a little crazy, because someone else might think that person is quite different. So, which is true?

Not only do we experience the people in our lives through our concepts of them, but we do the same thing with ourselves. We believe we are who we think we are. We have concepts of ourselves, and not only do we view ourselves through those concepts, but we are very good at finding evidence to support them.

Perceiving through our concepts deprives us of direct experience. Direct experience—whether of a tree, another person, or ourselves—is about seeing what is, as it is, in the moment, without preconceptions.

Ram Das once said, "If you think you're enlightened, go spend a week with your family."[1] I think we all know that when we spend time with our parents or siblings, we revert to behaviors we thought we were well past. Why is that? Because in our family of origin, we have such a thick web of concepts about each other and ourselves that we behave in ways consistent with that conceptual web. These are the people with whom it is most difficult to come to with an empty, fresh perspective, without the shroud of concepts.

67

So, part of the spiritual journey is about experiencing life as it is. That means being willing to set down the concepts as they arise and to come back to what's actually present—to experience directly.

If you turn on the television and see one of your favorite politicians—or one of your least favorite politicians—do you experience that person as they are? Do you hear what they are actually saying, or do you hear them through your concepts of them?

Obviously, the easiest encounters to experience directly are with things or people with whom we have no history, no prior narrative. But much of life is not experienced directly. Instead, we experience an illusion created by perceiving through our concepts.

Let's turn now to how our desires and fears affect our ability to see what is as it is. Imagine you are just getting to know a potential romantic partner. Are you experiencing that person as they are? If you desire a particular outcome, a particular type of relationship, you are probably focused on certain cues and certain responses. You are focused on how what they do and say makes you feel. You are not getting to know them. You are getting to know how they fit what you are looking for.

The same is true of fear. Imagine you are interviewing for a new job. The interviewer would be your boss if you are hired. Are you seeing this person as they are? Probably not. You are afraid of saying the wrong thing, of not making a good impression. You are focused on how the interviewer is judging your responses. Seeing people as they are requires letting go of our fears and desires. It involves being present, letting go of what might happen.

Finally, let's consider how our unprocessed emotions affect our ability to see what is as it is. As we discussed in Dealing with Uncomfortable Emotions, life hits our energy blocks created by unprocessed emotions. Our reactions to these blocks being hit are usually incommensurate with the triggering event. Sometimes great disturbance is created by what an objective bystander might consider a neutral event. We don't see the triggering event as it is; we see it as a "repetition" of the experience that we never fully processed.

Life is not an illusion. We encounter real people and real events. But we do not see them as they are. Our concepts, desires, fears, and unprocessed emotions create distorting lenses through which we perceive them. We live in an illusion created by these lenses. A key aspect of spirituality is the removal of these lenses.

CHAPTER 12

Self-Awareness Rather than Self-Improvement

M ost of us have been engaged in a lifelong project of self-improvement. We did not initiate this project ourselves. Most likely it was originally our parents who endeavored to foster our improvement. They were committed to our development in "positive ways." They probably wanted us to be good people, successful, respectful, and respected. Consequently, they continually gave us direction. Some of that direction had the desired effect and some did not. However, a major consequence was that we internalized their improvement project; we became focused on self-improvement.

The question arises: *why* do we want to improve ourselves? The first answer is that we think that if we were better, we would accrue more of what makes us happy. If I were a better person, people would like me more; I would have more friends; my relationships would be better. If I were more hardworking, I would be more successful. If I worked out more and ate better, people would find me more attractive. Most of us are walking around with an evolving list of how we need to improve. I need to smile more, inquire more often about others, be less angry, and be more punctual. Our program for improvement involves major and minor changes.

The second answer to why we want to improve ourselves is that if we were better, we would have less self-judgment. This is problematic. We judge ourselves because the ego mind says that we are not good enough; we need improvement. However, our focus on self-improvement reifies that we are not good enough, which is the basis for our self-judgment. Thus, self-improvement will never eliminate self-judgment.

What is involved in enacting our program for self-improvement? For the most part, it is similar to the way our parents approached it; we attempt to change our behaviors and our personality. An example of the former is remembering to smile more regularly in social situations. An example of the latter is being more thoughtful or supportive of others. There are several problems with this approach. First, you may have noticed that it does not work all that well. Second, it involves us in ongoing self-judgment. If I need to improve in this particular way, then I sit in judgment of myself. Am I doing better? Am I backsliding? We are engaging in self-judgment to end self-judgement. This is as effective as fighting for peace. Third, the program for self-improvement becomes an ongoing affirmation that I am not okay the way I am; I need to be different. It reflects a lack of self-acceptance and is part of the larger agenda of the ego mind that identifies what needs to happen in the future and what needs to be avoided in the future for us to be okay.

There is an alternative to all this. That alternative is to realize that we are not the ego mind, but rather we are the observer of what is going on in the mind. You may have noticed that the majority of the thoughts you have are not thoughts you chose to have; they simply arrived uninvited. Sometimes, people's self-improvement goals are to improve their thoughts, but that is really a lost cause because

71

we have little control over our thoughts, and it just puts us in judgment of our own minds.

So, when we realize we are not our minds, we are the witness of our minds, we recognize that we do not need to buy into the mind's self-improvement agenda. The mind says we will be okay when we are neater, when we are more punctual, when we are friendlier. We can simply notice this unhelpful advice and let it go. In noticing our thoughts rather than buying into the content of these thoughts, we come back to being present–knowing ourselves as consciousness. The witness, the consciousness that we are, does not need improving. When we are not in self-judgment, when we are not listening to the ego mind's agenda for being okay in the future, we *are* okay.

Does that mean we do not change? Well, as humans, we do change. However, the change occurs in a manner different from what the mind conceives. The mind conceives of change as resulting from our self-judgment. Self-judgment is the carrot and stick that motivates self-improvement. But as we discussed, that seldom works. Awareness, on the other hand, does produce change, but not necessarily the changes advocated by the ego mind. Being present, being aware and open, allows changes to happen. We evolve naturally in the atmosphere of (self) acceptance. If you were to go to a therapist, and Therapist A judges you and tells you how you need to change, while Therapist B is totally accepting, which therapist would be more useful? We know that the situation that supports change is one of acceptance and rather than judgment. The ideal therapeutic situation is one that supports us in seeing ourselves objectively without judgment. Witnessing the ego mind, letting go of adherence to its self-improvement program, creates such a situation.

Let's take an example. You want to lose weight, believing that if you were thinner, you would be happier (self-improvement). After a stressful day, you take out a quart of ice cream and eat a significant portion of it. This results in self-judgment, which makes you feel bad about yourself. When you feel bad about yourself, one of your coping methods is to indulge or overindulge in food. So, the cycle continues, and you fail to reach your self-improvement goal.

Now consider that instead of having a self-improvement goal, you work on self-realization. You commit to witnessing (observing without judgment) your emotional states and your eating behavior. You begin to notice that when you feel stressed or down you eat. You begin to have a space between the stressed or down feeling and the action of eating. Increasingly, perhaps not 100% of the time, you make a choice to handle these emotions in a different way. This is how self-realization can bring about change–change that does not derive from self-judgment and attempts at self-improvement.

The spiritual journey is about letting go of these messages from the ego mind, letting go of self-judgment and letting go of the need to improve. We already have plenty of negative results from our attempts at self-improvement. Instead, we can engage in the experiment of self-realization.

CHAPTER 14

The Trap of Success

There are many successful people in the world, in terms of financial situation, recognition, and achievement. But does this success translate into being joyful, loving, and peaceful? Does it eliminate fear and anxiety? Of course it does not. It cannot. The source of joy, love, and peace is within us, as are the causes of fear and anxiety. Success in the external world cannot change what derives from within us. This is a point discussed in other chapters, so I will not go into detail here. In this chapter, I focus on a trap that frequently ensnares successful people.

Let's take, for example, Sofia. Sofia built a successful business. Over the years, the business continued to grow. To manage the growing business, Sofia gradually increased her work hours. She is now working an average of six twelve-hour days a week. Sofia would like to spend more time with her family and friends and more time exercising, meditating, and engaging in activities she enjoys, but she does not feel she can spare the time from the business. Although Sofia experienced some health problems recently, she only takes time off when they are severe enough to prevent her from working. Her health problems have not prompted any lifestyle changes.

Why does Sofia live as she does, seemingly trapped in her business, trapped in her success? There are likely a number of reasons. First, being a successful businessperson is a large part of Sofia's self-concept. Although Sofia has all the financial resources that she and her family need, she has become attached to the ever-growing income and notoriety her growing business brings her. Sofia also sees herself as someone who looks out for her employees. Selling the business would be tantamount to abandoning them. So, Sofia is unable to make a change, whether by reducing the scope of the business, giving up some of the management responsibilities, or selling the business. It seems that the only thing that will bring about change in Sofia's involvement in her business is serious illness. Sofia is caught in the trap of success.

Let's consider a second example. Darnell is a writer. His first novel was a big success. That success led to the belief that he had to produce additional successful novels to show that he was a legitimate literary talent and not a flash in the pan. Over several decades, he wrote a number of novels. Enough of his works were successful, establishing him as a well-respected author. Each time he publishes a novel, he has to embark on an extended book tour. He doesn't really like the tours, and they are disruptive to his life. Now, comfortable financially and wanting to do some things he has been putting off, Darnell still feels a need to write additional books. He wants to show that "he's still got it" and that he is still relevant. He, too, is caught in the trap of success.

What is *the trap of success*? The most important component of the trap is identification with the successful endeavor, whether it is business, art, athletics, entertainment, medicine, law, or academia. As successful people, we build our self-concept around the successful endeavor. "Who would I be if I were no longer a successful _____?" Attachment to the benefits that accrue from that endeavor, such as money, recognition, respect, popularity, power, and influence creates additional pressure to continue. Further, the ego mind is always telling us that achieving more success, so that we get more benefits, will ultimately make us happier and reduce our fear and anxiety. Finally, the trap can involve a sense of responsibility to continue what we have created and to the people involved.

You might ask, "Why do call it a trap? This seems to imply something undesirable." Well, let's look at what often happens. Continued success gets prioritized over family, health, living one's life more fully, and spiritual evolution. So much of what one values gets put off or given short shrift. And what makes this a trap is the inability to make a change, even when one recognizes the need. We all share the universal desire to live in peace, love, and joy, free from fear and anxiety. This book is about making changes that bring us closer to that state. But the trap of success works against change. And the greater the success, the harder it can be to escape the trap.

But there is good news. First, success does not *require* falling into the trap. If we are doing, at all times, what fits in the present without attachment to results in the future, we can avoid this trap. We can walk away from our successful enterprise when it no longer fits. This does not imply that we just drop everything. Getting out of a business or changing our academic commitments might take time to unwind responsibly, but we do not need to be trapped and unable to make a change.

Second, the trap is created by the ego mind. It is built from thoughts such as, "If I can substantially increase the size of the business, I will feel secure financially" and "If I can write a couple more bestsellers, my reputation will be cemented; I will be respected and feel good about myself." However, if we are willing to witness these thoughts, instead of buying into them—and let them pass—we can return to the present and do what needs to be done. Seeing the trap and recognizing how we are trapped is the first step. We do not need to struggle to free ourselves. The trap is illusory. We only need to let go of the illusion.

CHAPTER 15

Aging

We all hold beliefs about aging, including what happens to the physical body and the mind as we get older. These beliefs tend to be embedded in our culture. However, we do not think of our ideas about aging as beliefs. Rather, we accept them as *truth*. We can always point to evidence of their veracity. Even though we witness tremendous variation in how individuals age, our beliefs remain unshaken. Our beliefs about aging tend to involve expectations of physical and mental decline and a lesser role in society. We have a whole story about what will unfold as we get older. If we encounter somebody who is in her nineties and is vital, happy, and contributing, we see that person as an exception. Our story about aging remains intact. But why do we hold onto this story? We do so because the story is useful to the ego mind. For the ego mind, expecting adverse events makes it feel more in control than if such events occur unexpectedly.

Let's look at the impact of our beliefs about aging. I invite you to do a thought experiment. Imagine that you are physically, mentally, and emotionally as you are now. The only difference is that you and everyone you know believe that you are 15 years younger. Would this change how you experience your life? I think it would change your experience in significant ways. It would change your idea of where you are in your life, how many years you have left, what you are capable of, and what you will be capable of in the near future. It would affect whom you see as your peers. It might affect what is still worth doing (e.g., starting a new job, buying a new home). It would also affect your interpretation of your experiences.

For example, if you forget something that you think you should have remembered, and you believe yourself to be 40, you might laugh it off. But if you see yourself as 55, you might consider it a "senior moment" or an indication of memory decline. If you have specific injuries at 50, you might engage in rehab and physical training to prevent the injury from recurring. However, if you are 65, you might see it as age-related decline and avoid activities that could provoke a recurrence.

When I was in my thirties and forties, I had a lot of lower-back problems. I often had such bad back spasms that my body was crooked. It was painful and disabling. Over the subsequent decades, my lower back has been much better. If this had happened in reverse, going from healthier to less healthy, I would likely have seen it as the effect of aging. But how does having a healthier and stronger back as a senior citizen fit into the aging story? Our beliefs about aging not only determine our expectations, but they also shape how we interpret our experiences.

So how do these expectations and interpretations affect our lives? Let's take a couple of examples. Imagine someone who has been active and athletic. At a certain point, she begins to expect accelerating decline. She has a couple of injuries in a short period of time, nothing serious, perhaps a muscle strain and some tendonitis (e.g., tennis elbow). Her beliefs about the relationship of her injuries to aging cause her to slowly make changes. She stops playing tennis, changes her aerobic exercise from running to walking, lifts lighter weights, and exercises with less exertion. These changes result in her feeling less strength. Now when she engages in uphill hikes, she tires more quickly and gets winded more easily, so she begins avoiding hiking uphill. You can see where this is going. The expectations and interpretation of aging affect what she does and how she sees herself. The changes in what she does affect her experience, which she further interprets as the effects of aging. It is a slippery slope.

The same can happen in other areas of life. Imagine someone who reaches 65 years of age and decides to retire. Once he is no longer working, he begins to feel less useful and less valued, as much of his identity was wrapped up in his work. His beliefs about age prevent him from taking up new long-term undertakings. He spends more time watching television and surfing the web. As a result, he feels less vital, capable, and useful. Again, we are on a slippery slope.

Our beliefs about aging also affect our expectations of how we will feel emotionally in the future. We tend to expect that we will be less happy and less satisfied with life as the "symptoms" of aging develop. But in fact, many of us who are 65 or older can look back and say, "Life has continued to get better. I am happier, less stressed, and more at peace than ever before." This is a significant realization! However, many who could say this still fear aging in the future. Our story about aging can be more powerful than our experience.

This leads to the question of how our lives would be different if we dropped our stories about aging and lived without the expectation of progressive decline and diminishing satisfaction. What if we experience life as it unfolds, focusing on the present instead of inventing the future? What is the downside of approaching each moment as a moment of possibility, as an adventure? There clearly is a downside to expecting decline and diminishment and then finding evidence to support it.

Up until this point, we have focused exclusively on giving up our stories about aging. There is another factor worth considering with respect to aging. In Chapter 7, "Dealing with Uncomfortable Emotions," we discussed how our unfinished uncomfortable emotions result in energy blocks. We expend energy avoiding these emotions. The more blocks and the larger the blocks, the more energy is tied up.

Most of us spend our entire lives acquiring energy blocks (not fully experiencing uncomfortable emotions) and growing those blocks (not fully experiencing what arises when those blocks are triggered). This way of dealing with our emotions, over time, makes aging a process of decreasing energy and, therefore, declining health and vitality. But the good news is that aging does not have to be this way. By regularly engaging in the practice of releasing our emotions, discussed in "Dealing with Uncomfortable Emotions," we can not only avoid adding to our energy blocks but also decrease the number and size of our existing blocks. Thus, we can use the challenging moments of life to increase, rather than decrease, our available energy.

Who will join me in the experiment of living without beliefs about aging? Of course, letting go of these long-held beliefs is not a one-time event. If and when these beliefs crop up, we let them go and come back to the present. Who will join me in exploring the possibilities created by releasing our emotions? We can be excited about life as it continues to unfold.

Q. Aren't our beliefs about aging supported by statistics?

A. Yes, they are, but the statistics do not make our beliefs true. These statistics reflect a population that holds negative beliefs about aging. As we discussed, these beliefs have an ongoing impact on how we live our lives and what we experience in our senior years. These statistics derive from a population that continues to acquire energy blocks from unprocessed emotions resulting in decreased energy and vitality. Ultimately, we must ask whether these statistics indicate what is hardwired into aging or what is changeable. I suspect that a lot less is hardwired than we believe, which is precisely why I propose the experiment.

CHAPTER 16

We Are All Dishonest and Controlling

Most of us think of ourselves as honest people. But what do we mean when we say that we are honest? We might mean that we do not make up major false stories and communicate them to others. We might mean that we do not engage in secret affairs if we are in a monogamous relationship. We might mean that we do not cheat financially. So, if we are not dishonest in these ways, might we still be dishonest?

Let's look at some examples. Someone asks me, "What are you thinking?" and I say, "Nothing." I may not want to share the content of my thoughts, because they are critical or because the timing is bad. Perhaps we were about to engage in an intimate moment, and my mind says, "If I share this now, it's going to ruin the moment."

What are some other ways we are not completely honest? We might give someone a compliment that is not sincere. We might tell someone we love the present they gave us even though we did not really like it. We might offer a false excuse for why we are late, missed a birthday, or cannot attend an event. And of course, there are our responses to the ever-popular question: "Does this make me look fat?"

Interestingly, most of us want a level of honesty from others, particularly those close to us, that we do not maintain ourselves. So why are we not more honest? Because these "white lies" are an attempt to control. In many cases, they are an attempt to get others to act in ways we want or to avoid them acting in ways we do not want.

Thinking of ourselves as controlling may seem strange. We usually consider people to be controlling if they are manipulative, threatening, or underhanded. But those are not the only ways of being controlling. We just discussed how we use small dishonesties to control, and there are other ways we attempt to control. Consider the following examples.

My partner wants me to do something with her that I really do not want to do. However, I do not say anything and just go along, because I do not want her to get upset. More accurately, I do not want to have to deal with her upset. My going along is an attempt to avoid her reaction. In general, not telling someone something is a way of controlling. Postponing telling someone something until the *right time* (to avoid an inconvenient reaction) can also be a way of controlling.

What is the person doing who is about to go on a date or out with friends and tries on six different outfits? He is likely trying to control some combination of how others see him and how he sees himself. Perhaps, we are in a group, and we say something to show how smart we are. In another group, we say nothing to hide our lack of knowledge of what is being discussed. Attempting to control how others perceive us is a significant part of our control efforts. We do not notice many of these actions (and inactions) because we view them as typical behavior. We are all controlling, and we are all dishonest. But why?

Control is a specific antidote to fear. I use *fear* to include both big and little fears. The one thing that makes us feel less afraid is feeling some measure of control. If we are regularly trying to control, we must be afraid a lot. But why are we afraid? We are afraid because the ego mind is constantly telling us what we must get and avoid to be okay. The natural reaction is fear–fear that we will not get what we want or need and fear that we will get what we do not want or what we seek to avoid. So, we are afraid, and when we are afraid, we attempt to control. Our need to control shows us our identification with and the dominance of the ego mind.

We might ask, is it working? How are we doing with our attempts to control? If we are honest with ourselves, we must admit that it is not going well. We are unable to control much of what we fear. The data are overwhelming. We have been trying to control people and situations for our entire lives. It would be delusional to believe that our efforts to control will succeed in the future.

So, we are regularly in fear. We are trying to deal with the fear by controlling. And our attempts to control are not working or at least not working well. The only way to deal with this situation is to work with the root of the problem. The root of the problem is the source of the fear–the ego mind. More specifically it is our identification with the ego mind that causes us to pursue the ego mind's list of what we need and what we need to avoid.

We have discussed the solution to this problem before– witnessing the mind. When we witness the mind, we notice how the ego mind keeps talking, keeps discussing this list. We do not have to buy into the list. We do not have to buy into the ego mind's plan for us to be conditionally okay in the future. In witnessing the mind, we do not struggle with the mind. The mind has its own nature, and we can witness it and allow the thoughts to pass. We know that we are the one who is aware of the mind's chatter; we are the consciousness. In witnessing the mind, we enter the present moment and are immediately free from the conditional promises and threats of the ego mind. We are okay *now*—free of the source of the fear. We have no need to control.

Let's consider one final point. When we witness the mind, it is not the ego mind's list that we are letting go of; it is the belief that the list represents what we need and need to avoid to be okay. When we let go of this belief, we may still engage with items on the list. For example, we may look for a new house or a new job. The difference is our relationship to the list item. We are now relaxed about it, free of fear. Our being okay is not conditional upon finding a new house or a new job. We *are* okay. We can be present, doing what is appropriate to do, in this case, looking for a new house or a new job. The items on the list were never the problem. The problem was that we bought into the proposition that our being okay would happen only in the future and only if we succeeded with the items on the list.

CHAPTER 17

The Self-Concept

As human beings, we are blessed with a powerful learning mind; the mind learns from experience. Consider all the things we learn between birth and two years of age. This learning is not the result of a deep commitment to learn. It occurs because of the nature of the mind. We learn essential skills like eating, drinking, and dressing ourselves. We learn how to walk and talk. As we grow older, we acquire more complex knowledge: mathematics, history, social norms, and how to use sophisticated tools. The mind is incredible; it never stops learning.

One focus of the mind is learning to keep us safe and comfortable. It remembers what made us feel unsafe or uncomfortable and what brought us happiness, contentment, and a feeling of well-being. An important product of this learning is the mind's construction of a self-concept. It constructs an idea of who "I am." This includes the roles we play. Early on we identify as a son, or daughter, sibling, or grandchild. We identify as students and progressively as a particular type of student with particular abilities and weaknesses. We come to know ourselves in terms of our activities and our proficiency in those activities, for example: athletics, art, music, and computer games

Besides identifying with our roles and abilities, our self-concept includes our attributes. Are we smart, silly, foolish, sensitive, strong, emotional or rational? Are we generous, supportive, or a good listener? We develop notions of ourselves that could be classified as both positive and negative. The self-concept is decades in the making and is the "self" we share with the world. But what is the function of the self-concept?

Sharing our self-concept with the world is one way the mind attempts to establish control. By defining how others see us, the mind is better able to predict and influence how others respond to us (at least in theory). The mind uses the self-concept to get more of what it wants and less of what it does not want. For example, when I was younger and entered into a new group of people, I often attempted to demonstrate at least one of three aspects of my self-concept, being smart, being athletic, or being a good dancer. Of course, it was necessary to put myself in the right contexts. I was not "smart" about all subjects. I was a good soccer player, but a poor swimmer. I was a good dancer to R&B, but had no particular abilities in square, country, or line dancing. The purpose of demonstrating my competence in one or more of these areas was to attract attention (without the vulnerability of initiating conversation) and ultimately to be valued and liked.

Sharing one's strengths is not the only way to use one's self concept. One might share one's weakness or incompetence, drawing attention and assistance from others who can enjoy feeling strong, competent, and helpful.

However, we not only create a self-concept and present it to the world, but we also defend it. If someone challenges an aspect of our self-concept, especially one that is core to "who we are," we defend it almost as if we were physically attacked. For example, if we believe ourselves to be generous and someone accuses us of being selfish, our fight-or-flight responses kick in.

The problem is that none of what constitutes our self-concept is who we really are. For many of us this is difficult to accept. We have spent so much of our life identified with our self-concept. I was a professor, but if I hadn't been, I would still have been me. If I had never been a skier or soccer player, I would still have been me. These attributes are just concepts, ideas about myself, not who I am. Our self-concepts change over time. Many of us probably have noticed that in our family of origin, years after we have been living independently, our parents or siblings still relate to us as "who we were", and we often revert to that self (-concept). But neither the self-concept we shared with others as children or the one we developed later in life is who we are. Who we really are is an unchanging presence. Being identified with our self-concept is like being identified with our clothes. It is what we cloak ourselves in, not who we are.

Another source of self-concept is the judgments we have of others. I spent a good part of my life trying not to be seen as foolish. I made many decisions to ensure that others did not see me as foolish. But where did this start? I probably judged others for being foolish, and this judgment was internalized as a potential judgment of myself. Avoiding being foolish was important as it avoided self-judgment and the (anticipated) judgment of others.

The spiritual journey is about letting go of the self-concept. It's realizing that we are not our roles or the attributes we have spent our lives trying to reify. The more we let go of the self-concept, the more we get in touch with who we really are. Looking back, I see how much time I spent trying to convince others that I was smart, athletic, attractive, or good. There is a real freedom in not needing to engage in such self-portrayal. When I experience the tendency to defend, support, or add to this self-concept, I can let go, knowing that it is not who I am. I do not have to work to maintain it.

Most people never consciously let go of their self-concept. As they age and face retirement, physical limitations, or other aspects of aging, it becomes a crisis. It's hard to maintain the idea that they are a lawyer, professor, contractor, or athlete if they have retired or developed physical limitations. Life gives us many opportunities to let go of the self-concept, but it requires awareness. Letting go of the self-concept is not a one-time event. We can free ourselves from identification with the self-concept, a creation of the mind, and know ourselves as who we really are.

CHAPTER 18

Humility that Matters

In our culture, being humble is considered a positive characteristic. Usually, humility is understood as speaking modestly about oneself, deflecting praise, and taking minimal credit for achievements and positive performance. Leaders or star performers often express humility by recognizing the contributions of collaborators and subordinates. Although being humble in this way is regarded as admirable, it does not have much impact on the quality of our lives. However, there is a deeper form of humility that is impactful. This humility is central to spirituality and is expressed in the sentence, "I, the individual self, cannot (did not) do it." By "individual self," I mean the self that we typically identify with, including the mind, body, and emotions. Let's unpack this notion of humility.

I will begin by discussing humility in the context of great achievements. People have created great paintings, music, architecture, scientific discoveries and have accomplished incredible physical feats. Can you or I do these things? Certainly not by just deciding, "I'm going to create a great painting," or "I'm going to write the next great novel." It's not clear that anybody ever created great work by deciding to do so. Many of those who accomplish extraordinary works recognize that this is something that comes through them rather than something they do. Mozart heard the music and wrote it down. Sure, he needed skills, but skills alone would not have been enough. Einstein had particular insights. Where did they come from? Not just from studying physics. There were many people who knew as much physics as Einstein, but they didn't come up with the theory of relativity. Great athletes sometimes describe themselves as "being in the zone." What does that mean? It means they are not in their mind, and the performance just seems to happen. Performing at that level is not something they can *make* happen. Great performances and achievements do not seem to be merely a product of hard work.

Of course, most of us might never produce great performances or achievements. Let's consider what our individual selves can and cannot do. If I cut my finger, can I make it heal? If I am looking for a romantic relationship, can I make that person appear? Can I make or keep myself healthy? Can I make myself rich or famous? The answer to all of these questions is, "No." I can do things that are supportive of the desired result or at least that do not prevent it from happening (keeping my finger clean, eating healthy food, investing), but I, the individual self, cannot make it happen.

So, why is it important to realize that I, the individual self, have little control and limited resources? It is important because it allows us to approach life differently. We can give up the myth that everything is a matter of what we do and do not do. How might our lives be different? Let me give a personal example.

As discussed in the introduction, the chapters of this book are revisions of talks that I have given in the meditation group that I lead. But I, the individual self, cannot and did not give those talks. I know how to prepare a talk or lecture. I've done it proficiently throughout my professional life as an educator and education researcher. However, I realized several years ago that if I just shared what *I know*, my meditation group talks would be limited by my individual knowledge and understanding. I wanted to do the experiment of getting my individual self out of the way and seeing what came through me. Towards this end, I decided to do no preparation for my talks. I show up each week with only a topic in mind and share what comes through me in the moment. This experiment was scary at first. But it has produced wonderful results. I am excited each week to see what comes through. I learn as much or more than any of the participants. It is a blessing, a blessing that only requires getting out of the way. Note that as I turn these talks into chapters, I use both *what I know* and any inspiration available to me as I am engaged in the process.

But let me share another bit of the experience. I have been giving these spontaneous talks for several years now, and the other members of the group and I have been benefiting from the teachings that result. Nonetheless, my ego mind still tries to intervene. Here is what that looks like. The meditation group sessions begin with a silent meditation. During the meditation, my mind frequently draws my awareness away from the breath. Sometimes it is my mind starting to figure out what to say. When I notice, I bring my awareness back to the breath. But why does this still happen? It is because the lack of preparation is uncomfortable for the ego mind. The ego mind is a planner, but I purposely have not planned, it seeks control, but it is not in control. As a result, there is fear that I will have nothing to say or run out of things to say quickly, that I will embarrass myself. However, I do not have to listen to the mind or buy into the fear.

Rather, I have learned to trust that there is something greater than my ego mind that requires only receptivity. I am the conduit.

I like the analogy of life being a river. The most compatible way to deal with life is to go with the river. If I am in a kayak, I can feel myself carried by the current. I can participate with the river (life) by staying aware and steering lightly to avoid rocks. But I, the individual self, am not choosing the path or the velocity. If on the other hand, I were to decide that I want to go straight down the middle of the river, it would be a tough ride. If I were to decide that I want to head upstream, it would be even tougher. But in life, how many of us regularly fight the current rather than enjoy the adventure of being carried by it?

So, how would life be different if we consciously said,

I, the individual self cannot do it. I have neither the control nor sufficient resources. Let me open to the power that animates life, a power that is far greater than my individual self. I can open to it, participate with it, be excited by it, and be grateful for it.

Can we give up resistance to life and participate in it? Can we trust the ride?

Q. We do make choices in our lives, don't we? Isn't that control? We make decisions about whom to marry and where to live.

A. First, let's examine the scale of our decisions. I can decide what to have for dinner, but I cannot decide, and I am not in control, of how well I digest it. I can decide whether or not to get a COVID vaccine, but I am not in control of whether I get COVID. And if I get COVID, I'm not in control of how severe the symptoms are, whether I get long COVID, or even whether I live or die. We can decide whether to marry our significant other, but the circumstances that allowed us to meet that person and to meet at the right time were not within our control. If we pay attention, we notice that the decisions we make are small relative to the enormous flow of life.

The second part of the answer relates to my teacher's term, "choiceless awareness." *Choiceless awareness* is about not resisting the river and participating with the current. When we are not identified with the content of our ego minds, struggling to get what it wants and avoid what it fears, we participate by being present and recognizing appropriate participation. Steering away from the rocks as we are carried down the river can be referred to as a choice, but it is choiceless awareness. It is that which is there for us to do in the moment.

I offer one more example from my life. My partner and I were looking to buy a house or apartment in the mountains for several years, but up until recently, we had been unsuccessful. We had looked at many properties, and they fell into two categories: either we did not like the place, or we liked the place, but it lacked one or more non-negotiable features. One afternoon, the realtor and I looked at a townhouse that was newly on the market. As I began to tour the townhouse, I had a good feeling. I liked the place, and it had no major drawbacks. Without wasting any time, I made an offer; we came to a negotiated price and signed a contract. During the several weeks that followed, many properties came on the market that seemed appropriate in terms of price, size, and location. My ego mind would comment that one or more of them might be a *better* place or be available at a *better* price. However, I trusted the process; I rode the current. I am at peace–noticing the mind's comments but letting them go. We completed the purchase of the townhouse. However, if

I had let my ego mind be in charge, I would have experienced internal conflict about whether we settled too soon and whether we could have done better.

I would be remiss if I did not mention a book that I read a number of years ago, *The Surrender Experiment*, by Michael (Mickey) Singer. It is an autobiographical account of Mickey's experiment in opening to where life takes him. But I have to admit that as inspiring as the book is, I was initially unsure about how to engage in the experiment in my own life. In hindsight, here is what I learned about getting started. Be prepared to start small. Begin by trusting your sense of knowing when opportunities present themselves. Recognize moments of insight that happen unexpectedly. Find moments to let go of your mind's menu of what you need and need to avoid and embrace the adventure of what shows up. If your experience is like mine, you will not notice the initial subtle changes in your relationship to the flow of life, but, at some point, you will recognize that significant changes have indeed occurred.

CHAPTER 19

Self-Judgment and Guilt

We all engage in self-judgment. We are critical of things we have done and things we have not done. Self-judgment can seem like a noble quality. It implies that we are introspective, taking responsibility for our actions and inaction, and committed to behaving better in the future. But does it work? Is it useful?

Imagine that you shared with a therapist something you did, and she responded judgmentally–telling you how wrong you were and how inappropriate your actions were. What effect would this have on your willingness to engage in self-examination in her presence and to share aspects of your past or present? Most of us would avoid doing so out of fear of further judgment. In fact, it is generally accepted among psychotherapists that creating a supportive, nonjudgmental relationship is key to the therapeutic process–key to creating the conditions for change.

One's relationship with oneself is much the same. If we engage in self-judgment, we are unlikely to look at ourselves openly. Self-judgment creates internal conflict and pain. It feels bad, and so we avoid self-exploration. Consider someone who is struggling with his weight. He frequently binges on food that he knows is not good for him. His reaction to these binges is self-judgment, self-condemnation.

Is this an internal environment in which he will openly examine what is going on? No, it makes him feel bad about himself—a situation that he wants to put behind him as quickly as possible. If he tends to eat in response to feeling bad about himself, a vicious cycle is created.

Self-judgment is the opposite of what we need. However, it seems to be deeply ingrained in us. Why? Many of us internalized judging from our parents. They criticized us when we misbehaved or when we failed to act appropriately. They expressed disappointment in and sometimes anger at our behavior. The result of these interactions was that we saw ourselves as flawed and in need of improvement. As we grew up, the judging parent became a feature of our self-talk. It seemed normal, even noble, to judge ourselves and expect improvement in the future.

Self-judgment is a feature of the ego mind. Our parents supported the development of this feature. The ego mind regularly engages in separating right from wrong and good from bad. The ego mind judges and sees our future well-being as contingent on self-improvement.

But where do the ego mind's concepts of right and wrong, good and bad come from? They come from our past. We have internalized concepts from our parents, grandparents, teachers, and clergy. We have also "learned" what is appropriate based on the responses of others.

Both major and minor incidents trigger the ego mind's self-judgment. However, if our self-judgments are strong enough, and if we hold on to them long enough, they can turn into guilt. Guilt can last a lifetime. You have probably heard people say, "I will never forgive myself for __." Is this helpful? Why do we do it? We do it in an attempt to see ourselves as "good people." If I reject the "bad" part of me, that feels like a positive. Yet, in doing so, a part of me rejects another part. Internal conflict is created and maintained. But inner conflict can never lead to peace, joy, or love– the qualities of being we ultimately seek.

So, what do we do about it? First, we need to understand that the judge–the source of our self-judgment–is the ego mind. If we let go of our identification with the ego mind and know ourselves as consciousness, we are letting go of the source of the problem. Consciousness does not judge. It is not the nature of consciousness. Consciousness witnesses. It "sees" without judgment.

Now, I can almost hear the objections. "I did this bad thing. I really hurt someone, and you are proposing that I just be okay with it?" First, realize that you, the consciousness, did not do it. The source of all of our unloving behaviors is the ego mind. Second, note that we regularly set up the offender (the ego mind) as the judge. Third, recognize that there is nothing to be gained from self-judgment and guilt. (We have already discussed the detrimental effects.) Does living for decades with guilt help the offended party? Of course not. Does it help you? No, so why do we consider it noble to hold on to our guilt? It is the ego mind's only option for dealing with the memory, for trying to turn a negative into a positive.

But will I be a good person without self-judgment? To repeat, the ego mind is the source of unloving behaviors. When we witness the mind, we let go of our identification with it. We come to know ourselves as the one who is aware of the mind, that is, we know ourselves as consciousness. Consciousness is the source of love and peace. Consciousness supports evolution.

We work with guilt by shifting to witnessing. Each time a thought of our guilt comes up, we witness it and let it pass. We do not fight with the mind. The thought was never the problem. The problem was our tendency to buy into the thought and accept it as a partial description of who we are.

We deal with self-judgment similarly. At the moment that a judgment threatens to manifest, we shift to witnessing. However, we will not always catch the judgment so early. If we do judge ourselves, we can witness the judgment. What may even occur is that we judge ourselves for something. Then, we judge ourselves for judging ourselves. And we might even judge ourselves for judging ourselves for judging ourselves. However, the moment we witness the last judgment, we are out; we have moved from the unconscious, judging ego mind to the nonjudgmental, witnessing consciousness. It does not matter how many unconscious steps we took; the moment we witness the last one, we are free. Consciousness is always that close–always available.

So, we experiment with letting go of guilt and self-judgment. This does not preclude us from taking responsibility for our actions and addressing issues that need to be addressed. Doing so does not require self-judgment. If I spoke harshly to someone, I can come back to them and apologize. I can do this while still accepting myself. I do not need to be unloving to myself to be loving to the other.

Q. If we do not judge, is there no right and wrong?

A. From a spiritual perspective, there is no right and wrong. Right and wrong are judgments based on our concepts. But letting go of the notion of right and wrong does not mean we do horrible things. Consciousness is a state of peace, acceptance, and love. We can trust what derives from consciousness. On the other hand, when people are judgmental, fearful, or struggling to get more in the outside world, all of which derive from the ego mind, they are capable of horrendous acts. So, knowing ourselves as conscious beings and letting go of our identification with the ego mind is the way to live from a loving place.

CHAPTER 20

The Source of Our Communal Problems

We all perceive significant communal problems at the local, regional, national, and global levels. Although people offer various explanations for these problems, I want to share a spiritual perspective. We have previously discussed how our identification with the ego mind creates problems for the individual. Here we explore how this identification is at the root of our collective problems as well.

What characteristics of the ego mind lead to these problems? The ego mind tells us we will be okay in the future *if* we acquire what it deems necessary and avoid what it fears. This is problematic because what one person or group wants may conflict with what another person or group wants. This leads to struggles that can become fights for dominance, territorial disputes, inter-group conflicts, and, in extreme cases, war.

Another related feature of the ego mind is its drive for control. The mind asserts that the more control and power we have, the more we can secure what we want and avoid what we fear. This leads to intense power struggles at every level of our collective life. Powerful individuals and groups seem to be obsessed with gaining more power, particularly power over others. This quest for ever-greater power is an attempt to address the desires and fears generated by the ego mind.

The ego mind is focused on the future, claiming that collectively we will be okay *when* we gain more power, wealth, or respect. The ego mind, which leads us as individuals to subjugate our own well-being in the present to potential achievements in the future (for example, overworking at the expense of our health), has an analogous effect at a collective level. This fixation on our future condition can result in a collective belief that the end justifies the means. Poor treatment of others, dishonesty, manipulation, and failure to follow laws and social norms can result from this attachment to the end goal. This is evidenced by the fact that humans, unlike other species, destroy the environment to get more of what they want.

This discussion can help us recognize that every characteristic we judge negatively in others exists within us. (See Chapter 16, "We Are All Dishonest and Controlling.") Perhaps our actions are less extreme, but the source of those actions is the same–identification with the ego mind.

Our collective problems will not be solved by the "right people" coming to power. We need a fundamentally different way of being and interacting. As long as the ego mind is in charge and as long as each group is struggling to get what it wants (sometimes at all costs), our collective problems will remain and perpetuate themselves. Real solutions will not be accomplished solely through external changes. We must work individually and collectively to know that we are not the ego mind, to value the present, and to recognize the inherent value of each of us. Merely hoping our side prevails is a weak and inadequate vision for our community, our country, and our planet.

Does this mean we should not get involved in elections and work for political candidates and parties? Does it mean that we should do only internal work? No, each of us should participate in life, including political life, as is appropriate for us. The question is, can we do this while being present and not believing that things will be okay in the future if we win? Can we participate without devaluing the political opposition? Can we contribute to quality in our collective lives by living consciously in each moment, even as we participate in political and social movements?

This discussion is not advocating inaction or solely focusing on internal work. Rather, it advocates an inside-out approach. The power of exemplary activists like Mahatma Gandhi and Martin Luther King Jr. stemmed from their internal state. They acted from love and presence, not ego. Can we do internal work so that our work in the world does not further contribute to the problem, so that we are part of a real solution? By cultivating awareness and presence, might we be able to navigate the complexities of the world while remaining grounded in love and compassion?

CHAPTER 21

Tranquilizing the Mind

W e are all addicts–not in the clinical sense, but we exhibit the underlying characteristics of addiction. Our addictive behavior is one way we deal with the ego mind.

There are many behaviors that we engage in addictively. Among them are eating, drinking, drugs, sex, gambling, video games, exercise, work, television, and surfing the internet. But what does it mean for them to become addictive and why does this occur?

The ego mind (as we have explored in various chapters) keeps us in a state of stress and struggle. It has an extensive list of what we need and what we need to avoid. Identifying with the ego mind and buying into its dictates keeps us busy, stressed, and in perpetual conflict with life as it unfolds. Further, the message that we will be conditionally okay in the future reinforces a self-image of not being okay in the present and needing self-improvement before we can be okay.

How do we handle this continuing stress, struggle, and negative self-image? We engage in behaviors that tranquilize or get us out of the mind… temporarily. So how does this work? Let's use alcohol as an example. After a day dominated by the ego mind, we feel tired, stressed, perhaps even beaten down. We have a few drinks and begin to feel less stressed, more laid back. This is a relief. This may be the best we have felt all day. In subsequent days, we again experience stress and struggle and remember what provided relief. So, once again, we have a few drinks. The more we use this source of relief, the more we become attached to its effects, and the more we depend on it.

But traditional sources of addiction, such as alcohol and drugs, are not the only sources of relief that we turn to. We overeat or snack frequently for short periods of pleasure. We engage with our computers, televisions, and phone screens to escape–anything to tranquilize the mind. People even use meditation in an attempt to tranquilize the mind. These tend to be the people who give up on meditation. Let's explore this use of meditation and also how meditation can be used to decrease or even end our addictive behavior, that is, our need to tranquilize the mind.

What does it mean to use meditation in an attempt to tranquilize the mind? Many people expect that meditation will provide relief from the stress caused by the mind. They believe that by focusing on the breath or repeating a mantra, the mind will be silenced. They may get occasional moments of relief as they focus on the breath or a mantra. However, over time, they deem meditation to be a failure, or they see themselves as failing at meditation. Why? Because their minds are regularly active during meditation. Thus, meditation does not meet their expectations; it offers little relief. These people are struggling with the mind. The experience of meditation is itself governed by the ego mind. Their minds are saying that they will be okay in the future if and when they develop the ability to stop the mind. This future does not arrive, and their self-image takes another hit from failing at meditation.

So, meditation is not a very effective way to *tranquilize* the mind. Unfortunately, alcohol and many other of our addictive behaviors tranquilize the mind more dependably. But although meditation falls short as a mind tranquilizer, it offers a real solution to the problems that lead to the need to tranquilize the mind.

The purpose of meditation is not to change the mind or silence the mind, but to de-identify with the (ego) mind. The mind has its nature. What the mind does is not a problem. The problem is that we identify with the mind, give it control, and believe its dictates. Meditation is the practice of witnessing the mind. If the mind is something we are aware of, *we* are not the mind. There are two powerful features of this perspective on meditation. First, relief from the stress created by the mind does not depend on changing the mind. It is available the moment we witness it, the moment we let go of our identification with the mind. Second, this perspective on meditation is not about finding temporary relief and then returning to the prior state. The practice of meditation teaches us to let go of identification with the mind, to free ourselves from the mind's dictates. This learning can be put into practice at any moment, not just during meditation.

CHAPTER 22

The Ego Mind's Override of Our Natural Gifts

In previous chapters, we have discussed the ego mind's agenda–its list of what we need/desire and what we need to avoid. In this chapter, we will explore natural gifts that seem to disappear when the ego mind is in charge.

One of our natural gifts is the innate wisdom of our physical bodies, a gift we share with animals. The body knows how to regulate breathing, regulate sleep, heal itself, and regulate food intake and metabolism.

The problem is that when the ego mind is in charge, it often overrides this innate wisdom. Let's take an example. You sit down for a nice meal. You are enjoying it and have eaten an amount that has satisfied your hunger, but the ego mind says, "Have some more. You'll get more pleasure." So, you have some more. You might even have a third portion. The result is that you eat more than you need, perhaps so much that you feel uncomfortable. If this becomes a pattern, it causes unneeded weight gain.

Contrast this with animals. There are no obese animals in natural settings. Animals do not eat beyond what they need and certainly not to the point of discomfort. Given the availability of food, they eat until their bodies say that they have had enough. Humans have the same regulatory mechanisms, but we put the ego mind in charge, and it overrides them. It seeks additional pleasure.

When an animal gets tired, it rests. When a human being gets tired, the ego mind often says, "You have more things to do; keep going" or "You are having fun (watching television, or out with friends), keep going." And so, we ignore the body's signal to rest.

Similarly, we override the signal to sleep. After overriding sleep signals for years, many people wind up regulating their sleeping and staying awake with medication. Animals do not need sleeping pills and neither, in most cases, do humans, *if* we listen to our bodies.

These important regulatory mechanisms that we share with animals are a gift of nature. However, the ego mind frequently overrides them. We do not hear the quiet signals of the body telling us what to eat and not eat, when to eat and stop eating, when to rest, and when to sleep. The louder messages from the ego mind have drowned out these crucial signals.

But we humans also have a higher-level gift–the gift of intuitive knowing. Intuitive knowing is a knowing that is immediate and spontaneous. But we are so used to taking direction from the ego mind that most of us are not aware of this ability. Intuitive knowing is the kind of knowing that we see in great composers, great artists, great writers, great athletes—the ability to go beyond the mind and be a receiver, be a conduit of what's available. Mozart heard the music and wrote it down. Does that mean we can all be Mozart? Probably not. But we all have the same instrument, the same receiver. However, we have lost track of it because we've put the ego mind in charge.

Let me refer back to a personal example that I discussed earlier in this book. The chapters of this book were derived from talks I gave in the meditation group that I lead. A few years ago, I decided not to prepare for these talks. I made this decision to allow intuitive knowing to come through. And what did the ego mind do? It panicked. It said things like, "What are you doing? You might have nothing or very little to say. You're going to embarrass yourself in front of the group. At least, prepare a little bit." This is how the ego mind responds when it is removed from being in charge. It has no access to what it does not know. It resists what it cannot control.

So, by putting the ego mind in charge, we have overridden both the low-level ability that we share with animals and the high-level ability of intuitive knowing. You might be wondering, "Can I get these abilities back?" The first part of the answer is, "They have never been lost." They have merely been overridden—just as the stars are not visible when obscured by the sun. The voice of the ego mind has been so loud that it has drowned out the voice of the body and the voice of the intuition. Regaining access to these subtler but powerful voices is a process. The first step is recognizing the problem. But what does the solution look like?

We begin to be aware of the ego mind as it is overriding messages from the body. It is easier to regain access to the voice of the body than the voice of intuition. The latter is subtler and likely less familiar to us. We observe messages like the ones previously discussed, "Eat more." "Eat this, you'll get pleasure from it." "Don't rest, you still have work to do." "Don't go to sleep, you're having such a good time."

As we become aware of these messages from the ego mind, we realize that we have been giving control to the ego mind, and we begin to choose to listen to the voice of the body. We begin to listen to its regulation of food, rest, and sleep. The key to this process is listening. As we listen, the voice of the body becomes clearer.

As we said, the voice of intuition is even more subtle. It requires even greater listening, even greater receptivity. Initially, we may be unsure if that faint whisper is actually the voice of our intuition. As with much of what we have discussed, it requires experimentation, having the courage to follow what *might* be intuition. It requires learning to discern the soft voice of intuition from the other voices. Listening to intuition is part of going with the flow of life rather than resisting it.

So, we can regain access to these inborn gifts, the voice of the body and the voice of intuition. It requires witnessing the ego mind, noticing its messages and letting them pass. The receptivity, the listening required contrasts with the ego mind's attempt to make things happen, to control. We can experiment with letting go of the doer and being the receiver.

Q1. Doesn't the ego mind sometimes give positive advice?

A1. The mind is a useful *tool*. It can be very helpful. Perhaps it learned to eat wild-caught salmon as opposed to farm-raised. Perhaps it learned to eat all colors of vegetables. These are helpful contributions of the mind. The *ego mind* is the condition of putting the mind in charge of making us okay. The mind is a useful tool. It is ill prepared to be in charge. It is not who we are. When it is in charge, many ineffective aspects of living occur, including losing access to the voice of the body and the voice of intuition. So, let's use the mind, but let's give up the misconception that we are the mind.

Q2. Don't we often use the mind in conjunction with intuition? Didn't Mozart use the mind to write down the music he heard?

A2. Yes. As we just discussed the mind is a useful tool. We often call on the mind to support initiatives of intuition. I used my mind in editing my talks to turn them into chapters. Even during the talks themselves, I used the mind, although trying to separate out the specific contributions of intuition and the mind would be difficult and not useful.

CHAPTER 23

What We Really Want

If I asked you, "What do you *really* want?" how would you answer? You might say that you want a house at the beach, a new relationship, to write a bestselling book, a grandchild, or to win the lottery. If I then asked you *why*, you might respond that it would make you happy or feel more secure.

But who is offering these two responses? It is the ego mind. The ego mind consistently identifies external changes that ostensibly will make us feel happier or more okay in the future–thus, the first response. But the ego mind also approaches life in a way that explains the second response–the *why*. To discuss this, we need some background.

Life exists as sets of polarities, birth and death, inhalation and exhalation, night and day. However, the ego mind tries to separate these polarities to get one half and avoid the other. It wants pleasure but not pain, success but not failure, happiness but not sadness. However, one cannot get half of a polarity. One cannot have the head side of a coin without the tail side. Let's take an example of a predicament that the ego mind puts us in. The ego mind tells us that if we find someone we truly love, we will be happy. We meet such a person, fall in love, and establish a relationship. However, what comes with this feeling of "This person makes me happy," is a fear of losing the relationship. Although the ego mind continually tries to get half of the polarity and avoid the other half, it never succeeds. Returning to our original responses, nothing can give us happiness without sadness or fear. Nothing can give us security without insecurity.

So, what *do* we really want? Alas, most of us do not have an answer. So far in the book, I have maintained that we all want the same things: joy, love, and peace. However, simply asserting this is inadequate, because I have not explained what I mean by those terms.

Please keep the following three points in mind as we continue this discussion. First, although I have highlighted three conditions— joy, love, and peace, they are actually aspects of a single state. Second, this state cannot be described in words. At best we can point towards the experience of that state. Third, in order to discuss these three aspects, we need to suspend our common usage of the terms. I will try to explain what these terms mean in *this* context.

Let's begin with joy. *Joy* does not refer to an emotion. If joy were an emotion, it would be part of a polarity, and we have already discussed the impossibility of getting half of a polarity. Emotions come and go; they can be both positive and negative. Joy refers to a state of appreciating life and experiencing well-being. It doesn't matter whether we are at the birth of a child or grandchild, or the death of a loved one. It doesn't matter whether we just won the lottery or are going through bankruptcy. Joy is not altered by the events of our lives. Ask yourself whether you have had an experience of joy that was not tied to any particular event; you just felt joy, perhaps only briefly. If you have had this (possibly fleeting) experience, the seed has been planted for what we are discussing.

Whether you can or cannot recall such an experience, pay attention for it.

Now let's talk about *love*. Here, we are not talking about a bond with another person, nor about a response to affection or generosity from someone. We are talking about a state of loving, a state in which love flows from within spontaneously. Can you recall such an experience when you felt love unrelated to any event or person? Whether you can or cannot recall such an experience, pay attention for it.

And finally, peace. Again, we are talking about a spontaneous experience unrelated to a particular life event. Consider this image. Imagine a beautiful lake. The water is completely still. It is an image of peace. Someone throws a stone into the water. There are a splash and ripples. Is the peace gone? I would maintain that it is not. The peace is not just the stillness of the water, but also how the ripples created by the splash diminish and dissipate. The water comes back to stillness. Likewise, the peace that we are discussing is not disturbed by the events of our lives. Have you experienced peace? Perhaps it was a moment in which you just stopped, took a deep breath, and relaxed. A feeling of peace came over you. Pay attention for such moments.

So, where are we in our discussion of what we want? Remember, this is not meant to be a discussion of three different states of being, but rather one state, a state that we could describe as joyful, loving, and peaceful–although any description would be inadequate. It is a state that requires us to be relaxed and present, that is beyond the mind and is beyond polarities. It is a state that is unaffected by life events–it cannot be improved. What if we could be in that state more? Who would not want to live in that state?

This is a difficult discussion to have because of the inadequacy of verbal description and limited awareness and experience of this state. Think about young children, excited by life–present and loving. Events disturb them, but they bounce right back to the state just described. Can we get back to this state *consciously*? If so, how?

Consider this analogy. We are growing vegetables from seeds. We plant the seeds. Then we watch carefully for the first tiny shoots. We nurture those shoots as they grow into seedlings and then mature plants. In this chapter, we are planting seeds of this state of being. Watch for the shoots–subtle little experiences. Nurture these shoots through relaxation, meditation, receptivity, and being present. Create the right conditions through letting go of identification with the ego mind and by releasing unprocessed emotions.

CHAPTER 24

What Is Not Changed by Our Spiritual Work

M ost of us embark on a spiritual journey to create a more peaceful life and to have a more loving relationship with ourselves and others. However, after a period of walking the spiritual path, many of us become frustrated. That which was supposed to change does not seem to have changed. Our frustration might be expressed in the following ways:

> *My spiritual practice should make me more loving and accepting, but I still find myself often judging people.*
>
> *My spiritual practice was supposed to make me love and accept myself, but I still have thoughts of not being good enough, smart enough, attractive enough, or lovable.*
>
> *After all my meditation and engagement with spiritual teachings, I still frequently get angry and hurt, often in response to little things.*

So, what is going on? Does this mean that our spiritual practice is not working? No, it is confusion about who or what is expected to change and what does not change.

Let's start by examining the first expression of frustration, "My spiritual practice should make me more loving and accepting, but I still find myself often judging people." The question is, who is judging? It is the ego mind that judges and has always judged. It is in the nature of the ego mind to judge. We do not engage in spirituality to change or improve the ego mind. We do not engage in spirituality so that the ego mind will produce kinder thoughts.

Likewise, who is generating self-rejecting thoughts? ("… I still have thoughts of not being good enough, smart enough, attractive enough, or lovable.") Again, it is the ego mind. The ego mind is focused on self-improvement, not self-acceptance (see Chapter 13, "Self-Awareness Rather than Self-Improvement"). It says that you will be okay and more lovable when you are better, smarter, or more attractive. This again is the nature of the ego mind. We do not engage in spirituality to make the ego mind more self-accepting. The ego mind has a whole agenda about what you need to do to be different in the future in order to be okay, happier, or at peace. It is the only way the ego mind knows how to function.

The problem is that we have a concept of what a spiritually evolved person is like–loving, peaceful, self-loving. Therefore, we are frustrated by the content of our thoughts when they do not fit with our concept of being "spiritually evolved." However, the ego mind does not need to change, and likely will not, through our spiritual transformation. The ego mind has its nature. What does change is our relationship to the ego mind. We learn to witness the mind. By doing so we give up our identification with it. If we are not identified with it, it is not in charge. We know ourselves as the consciousness. The ego mind can talk. We do not have to listen.

Many years ago, I listened to a recording of a talk by Ram Dass. His comments were colorful and germane to this discussion:

Even after many years of psychoanalysis, after teaching psychology, working as a therapist, after taking [psychedelic] drugs for many years, being in India, being a yogi, having a guru, meditating for eighteen or nineteen years now — as far as I can see I haven't gotten rid of one neurosis. Not one. The only thing that has changed is that while before these neuroses were huge monsters that possessed me, now they're like little Shmoos that I invite over for tea.[2]

The point is that the ego mind and the thoughts it generates are not a problem. The problem is identifying with the ego mind, putting it in charge, and being seduced or frightened by its messages. The ego mind likely will not change, but our relationship to it can.

What about the third frustration, "After all my meditation and engagement with spiritual teachings, I still frequently get angry and hurt, often in response to little things." This raises a different issue—our *reactions*. Where do these reactions come from? As described in Chapter 7, "Dealing with Uncomfortable Emotions," we have stored as energy blocks emotions that were not completed and released. Life events, including our own thoughts, can trigger a reaction by hitting these blocks. As long as we have anything in us to get hit, it will get hit. When a block gets hit, it creates a disturbance. We have no choice; the disturbance is automatic. However, we do have a choice about what we do with that disturbance. One choice we can make is to engage in the releasing practice described in Chapter 7.

So, if we diligently engage in this practice, what changes and what remains the same? What changes is that our energy blocks are diminished in size and number rather than increased. As a result, we will likely have fewer reactions, and some of the reactions that we

119

have will be less intense. What does not change is that we continue to have reactions when our blocks are hit.

I heard someone say (I believe it was based on something the Buddha said), "The anger of an enlightened master is like writing on water." There are two important aspects to this statement. First, it did not say that the enlightened master has no anger. Anger is a natural human response. However, the second point is that it is "like writing on water." It passes immediately, leaving no trace. If the master has released all of her energy blocks, there is no disproportionate reaction. And if she can witness it, remain established in consciousness, it passes quickly and completely.

To conclude, having unloving or judgmental thoughts (about ourselves or others) and having emotional reactions are not indications that our spiritual work is ineffectual. We have explored how and why these are natural and in no way inconsistent with spiritual transformation. Rather the transformation is reflected in our changed relationship to our thoughts and emotions.

CHAPTER 25

Meditation

Most people in western cultures engage in meditation as a way
to relax and reduce stress. There is nothing wrong with that. It is
certainly one of the healthier choices people can make, and it can
indeed reduce stress, at least temporarily. But meditation is not just
about relaxation. It is a key spiritual practice.

Spirituality involves a paradigm shift in the way we live. The old
paradigm has been our reality for most of our lives and is based on
identifying with the ego mind. This identification puts the ego mind
in charge. It endeavors to take care of us in the only way it knows
how. It says, "I will be okay when I get the things I want and avoid
the things I do not want or fear." The ego mind focuses us on the
future and never on the present moment. It promises a future state
that never arrives. We can never get all these external factors lined up
the way we want. The ego mind puts us in a condition of stress and
struggle as we try to get all that we want and avoid all that we fear. It
continually affirms that we are not okay *now*. We will only be okay in
the future when we get what we want and avoid what we do not want
or fear. The promise of being okay in the future, although seductive,
will never be realized. Recognition of this fact leads to consideration

of an alternative paradigm, specifically the spiritual paradigm we have been discussing.

The spiritual paradigm involves the realization that we are not our minds. We are consciousness. Unlike our minds, which are constantly changing, we, the consciousness, are unchanging. At some level, we know this. If we say, "When I looked in the mirror fifteen years ago, I saw a younger-looking face than I see now," the "I" refers to the same being in both cases. There is a continuity of *I*, in spite of the physical changes we observe.

As we have explored in previous chapters, we can be aware of the mind and its activity. "My mind is so busy thinking about my presentation tomorrow." "I've got this song stuck in my mind." "I keep having fearful thoughts about my upcoming operation." If I am aware of my mind, I am *not* my mind. *I* am the consciousness, the awareness. The mind is an object of consciousness. Everyone is aware, as the quotes above suggest. The spiritual paradigm involves being aware that we are aware—that we are the consciousness.

The spiritual paradigm also rests on knowing that what is real is the present. The past does not exist except in our thoughts and memory, and neither does the future. Being okay can only happen in the present. When we are absorbed in the present moment, we *are* okay. Let's examine this last claim. Someone who is totally awed by a sunset over the ocean or a mountain vista is okay. Someone who is totally absorbed in dancing, skiing, painting, or having a massage is also okay. We have had this experience. When we are totally absorbed in the present moment, we get a break from the mind's chatter about the past and the future. We experience a sense of well-being. For most of us, absorption in the present moment is occasional and dependent on particular events or activities. Spirituality involves learning to live each moment absorbed in the present unconditionally–not dependent on events and activities. We can always *be* in the present moment.

You might ask, "Does that mean we never make plans?" No. When we are making plans, we are totally absorbed in *that* activity. The difference is we are not living for the future. We are not sacrificing being okay now for some promise of being okay later. Putting money away for retirement is different from hating work for 40 years with the promise of being happy in retirement.

As we discussed, in the old paradigm, the ego mind is in charge. The mind has a particular facility. It "learns" from the past and uses what it has learned as it encounters future challenges. This is the way the mind works, and it will not change. Changing paradigms is not about changing how the mind operates or what it thinks. The problem with the old paradigm is not the content of the ego mind, but rather *identification* with it. By identifying with the ego mind, we give it the responsibility for making us okay. It does so in the only way it knows how. It uses the past to sort experiences based on memories of whether they made us feel more or less okay. It uses this sorting to try to control which experiences we have and do not have in the future. The ego mind is well-intentioned; it is trying to take care of us. However, as we discussed, its efforts are actually keeping us from being okay.

How we change this is quite simple. We realize that we are not the mind. We realize that we are the consciousness; we are aware of the changing content of the mind. The content of the mind is not a problem. I like the analogy of watching a movie. If we are watching a movie, it does not matter if the content is tragic, funny, sad, scary, touching, or thrilling. We are the ones watching the content and are okay watching diverse content. Sometimes a movie watcher will say, "That was a great movie. It was so sad that I had a good cry." If we decided we needed the content to be a certain way, we would be in conflict with the movie as it is and would not be okay. Similarly, if we are observers of our experiences in life, we do not need life to show up in a particular way for us to be okay.

So, the spiritual paradigm involves knowing ourselves as consciousness and giving up identification with the mind. It involves being fully present and realizing that the past and future are constructions of the mind. The challenge is that we have practiced the old paradigm for the vast majority of our lives. The good news is that we have a specific practice for establishing ourselves in the spiritual paradigm, *meditation*. Following are directions for the most common form of meditation.

Begin by sitting with the spine erect. (If you are physically unable to sit, you can lie flat or adapt as you need.) Relax the body. Rest your hands on your thighs, eyes gently shut. Begin to pay attention to the breath. Watch it enter and exit the body, and notice the pause between breaths. This is done without trying to change or control the breath. You can focus on the sensation of the breath entering and exiting the nostrils, observe the rising and falling of the diaphragm, or follow the breath as it fills up the chest and abdomen and then recedes. Note that there are other forms of meditation (e.g., repeating a mantra). The discussion that follows will apply as well to those forms.

When we are sitting in meditation, our minds inevitably wander; one moment we are observing the breath, and the next moment, we are thinking about something and are no longer observing the breath. Sometimes we notice quickly that the mind has wandered, and sometimes we may be lost in thought for a while. When we notice we gently bring ourselves back to observing the breath. We don't fight with the mind, and we don't judge ourselves for the distraction. But what if we do react by judging ourselves? We notice that we judged ourselves, we don't judge ourselves for judging, and we return to observing the breath.

One question that I find seldom discussed is why we focus on the breath (or repetition of a mantra). Focusing on the breath or a mantra gives us an anchor for our attention. My experience is that the anchor helps us be aware when thoughts come. It is easier to notice the disruption of our focus on the breath than to just notice the arrival of a thought. After all, we are used to having thoughts arrive without noticing their arrival. Noticing a thought that threatens to distract us or distracts us from our focus on the breath is the process by which we observe the mind (i.e., witness our thoughts).

To me, focusing on the breath has another subtle advantage. Breathing is an amazing phenomenon. It happens mostly without our awareness, and it self-regulates. Thus, for the most part, it is not under conscious control–but it can be. If I say, "Take a deep breath. Hold it. Now exhale," you control your breathing. In meditation, we get to experiment with being aware of a process that takes place normally without our awareness. It is an interesting experiment in consciousness to observe the breath without controlling it. It is not so easy to do. Initially, you may find that when you focus on the breath, you immediately begin to control it. This experiment can give us an additional experience of knowing ourselves as the consciousness.

Some people believe that in meditation, you should try to empty your mind. This works as well as *trying* to get to sleep–not at all. Consider this analogy. You are by a pond. There are ripples in the pond, so you move your hands across the surface of the water in an attempt to smooth out the ripples. Of course, you create more disturbance in the water. It is the same with the mind. Anything you do to calm the mind will create more disturbance. The pond can only become calm on its own. The mind is the same way, so trying to empty the mind is counterproductive. In meditation, we do not struggle with the mind. We merely observe it.

So why do we meditate? How does it support us in moving from the old paradigm to the spiritual paradigm? To recap, we said that the spiritual paradigm "involves knowing ourselves as the consciousness and requires giving up identification with the ego mind. It involves being fully present." Let's take these two points in order. When we meditate, we observe the mind. Observing the mind strengthens our knowing that we are the consciousness. If we are observing the mind, we are the observer, the consciousness, and not the mind. Second, meditation is practice being in and returning to the present moment. When we observe the breath, we are observing what is happening now. What is more present than our breath? We cannot breathe in the past. We cannot breathe in the future. As the breath is coming in, that is the present. As it is going out, that is the present. The space between breaths, that is the present. When we are distracted, we are not in the present moment. But the instant we notice that we are distracted, we are aware of what is happening now.

The most common misconception that I hear is, "I'm just not good at meditation." What they usually mean is that they spend considerable time distracted. Thus, they are "failing" to observe the breath. This is the ego mind talking, a remnant of the old paradigm. Nobody is good or bad at meditation. It is a practice. We benefit by practicing. Being distracted and bringing ourselves back to observing the breath is not an inadequacy; it *is* the practice. We have a mind. It distracts us. It talks to us both during meditation and throughout the rest of our day. Meditation is learning to notice that the mind is talking and to let it go. We are not the ego mind, and the contents of the ego mind will not make us okay. The more we practice noticing that the mind is talking and bringing ourselves back to the breath, the more we are able to do so throughout our day. So, noticing we are distracted in meditation is not failure, it is an essential part of the practice.

The mind can co-opt our meditation practice. It can tell us that if we meditate regularly, we will get better, more peaceful, more content. But this is the mind imposing the old paradigm of getting relatively better in the future. Here we see again the nature of the mind. Meditation is not about getting better in the future; it is about accessing who we are *now* and what is present *now*. The instant we observe the mind, we know ourselves as the consciousness. In that instant, the focus on the future drops away, and we are present. What we seek is available to us and experienced now.

So how does meditation give us what we seek? The instant we are present, observing our breath, there is a quality of being that does not exist in the old paradigm. In the old paradigm, we are busy and stressed trying to get what we desire and avoid what we fear. We are constantly in conflict with life because it fails to show up according to our desires. This new quality born of presence can be described in multiple ways. It is accepting and peaceful; nothing needs to be changed. We are not in conflict with what is now. There is a feeling of being okay, content. Might there even be an experience of love and joy?

You should not take my word for any of the effects of meditation. Conduct your own experiment. What do you experience as you are in the present moment? But watch out for your mind's attempts to *judge* your progress.

If meditation only produced these effects during the relatively brief time we allot to our meditation practice, it would not be of great value. But I began by claiming that meditation is a "key spiritual practice" and suggested that it is instrumental in helping us drop the old paradigm and live in the spiritual paradigm. How this works is very simple. By knowing ourselves as the consciousness and not the mind, we can observe the mind at any time. For example, if my mind says, "I would be happier if my partner were more ___ or less ___," I can notice that my mind is talking from the old (failed) paradigm and let the thought pass. In the past, I would have automatically bought into the message. Now I can see it as the mind's unproductive messaging. Likewise, meditation helps us to recognize when we are not in the present moment and return to it. I am trying to arrive at a meeting on time, but I have cut it close. The traffic light turns red just before I pass through the intersection. In the past, I would have been irked by the light turning red, and my stress about arriving late would have increased. Now, I notice that I am about to have a reaction. I take some calm breaths and use this break in my commute to be in the present moment, to be at peace. These subtle but powerful results of meditation impact our lives moment by moment.

I started by stating that meditation is not just about relaxation, but meditation and relaxation have an important relationship–a bidirectional relationship. It is helpful to relax our bodies and our breath before we begin our meditation practice. We generally create tension in both as we attempt to exert control over some aspect of our lives. Relaxing is preparation for moving into a space of being present with no need to change anything. But relaxation is also a *result* of meditation, not just because we are sitting quietly taking a break from our day, but because the de-identification with the ego mind frees us from the stress of constantly pursuing what it tells us we want and avoiding what it tells us we fear. This bidirectional relationship also exists as we bring meditative awareness to our daily lives, establishing ourselves in the spiritual paradigm.

CHAPTER 26

Getting Started

Everything we have discussed in the book is about changing the paradigm of how we live our lives. Although we can describe this paradigm shift in simple ways, knowing how to put it into practice in the moment can be elusive. Only experience can produce this knowing, yet it seems we need knowledge to begin practicing the new paradigm.

To review, the paradigm that we have been living in is one in which we are identified with the ego mind. The ego mind sorts through our past by identifying events that seemed to make us more okay and those that seemed to make us less okay. It impels us to seek more of the former and avoid the latter. As we have observed, this approach to life is not very effective. It is impossible to consistently get what the ego mind wants and avoid what it does not want. Trying to manage all these factors causes us stress and creates a situation where we are never truly okay. Rather, being okay is a future state contingent upon controlling these factors.

Realizing that the paradigm we have been living in does not give us what we truly want (peace, love, and joy), we begin to explore an alternative. The alternative that we have been discussing involves letting go of our identification with the ego mind and recognizing ourselves as consciousness.

The simple way to talk about consciousness is to point to the fact that we can observe our thoughts, feelings, and bodily sensations. If we can observe our thoughts, feelings, and bodily sensations, we are not our thoughts, our feelings, or our bodies. We are the subject aware of all of these objects of consciousness. We are consciousness.

But we have always been aware. When I say, "I can't get that song out of my head," or "I had this dream last night," I am indicating that I am aware of what is going on in my mind. We do not need spiritual teachings or practices to become aware. What is different in this new paradigm is being *conscious that we are conscious*, which allows us to know ourselves as the consciousness.

However, returning to the point made at the start of this chapter, living this new paradigm can be tricky. The change that we are discussing is both subtle and powerful, and its subtlety can make it difficult to grasp.

If I say, "Witness sensations in your body," you will likely be able to do so without difficulty. Bodily sensations are easily observable. But, if I say, "Witness your thoughts," you will likely find it more difficult. Likewise, if I say, "Witness your emotions," you may struggle with this directive. Observing thoughts and emotions is more subtle. You might even wonder, "Am I doing it?"

We are used to having thoughts. They often arrive uninvited. Intentionally witnessing our thoughts is different. You might wonder, "Am I thinking, witnessing my thought, or having a thought about my thought?" Similarly, distinguishing between experiencing an emotion and witnessing the emotion can be difficult. When people embark on the practice of witnessing emotions (described in Chapter

131

7, "Dealing with Uncomfortable Emotions"), they often struggle with how it differs from what they normally do. Someone grieving the loss of a loved one might ask, "I know that I am sad, so is that witnessing my emotion?" Because we are used to being absorbed in our thoughts and emotions, the subtle shift to witnessing them can be elusive. We need some way to begin–some way to know that we are practicing the new paradigm, practicing witnessing our thoughts and emotions. That is where specific techniques can be helpful.

We learn to witness our thoughts through meditation. In meditation, we give the mind an anchor, most commonly the breath. The breath involves a bodily sensation, which, as we said, is easier to witness than thoughts. Directions for meditation generally encourage us to focus on a particular sensation of the breath, such as the feeling of the breath entering and leaving the nostrils or the expanding and contracting of the chest. This specificity of focus takes further advantage of our ability to witness bodily sensations.

But how does this help with witnessing our thoughts? By focusing on the breath, we become aware of thoughts taking us away from that focus. Thus, the breath serves as a backdrop against which we notice the arrival of a thought. Do we always notice the first thought that comes? No. Sometimes we spend seconds or minutes caught up in our thoughts before realizing that our current thought is taking our focus away from the breath. This is not a problem. Each time we notice our thoughts taking us away from the breath, we deepen our ability to distinguish between thinking and witnessing our thoughts.

Note that other meditation techniques also use an anchor, such as repeating a mantra.

Now let's turn to the challenge of witnessing our emotions. Recall the example of the person who asked, "I know that I am sad, so is that witnessing my emotion?" The answer is "No." This person is describing the experience of being consumed by sadness and identifying with it. Consider this analogy for the difference between being sad and witnessing sadness. You are watching a movie. If you observe the main character experiencing sadness, you are witnessing. If it stirs something in you and you become emotional, you *are* sad.

Although this distinction is easy to make with respect to watching a movie, it is less clear for emotions that arise in our daily life. Here again we use a technique that involves witnessing bodily sensations, the practice described in Chapter 7. In that practice, we observe the physical sensations of the emotion. This helps us move from being consumed by and identified with the emotion to witnessing it. As we focus on the physical sensations of the emotion, we see the emotion as present in our body, perhaps intensifying, changing in sensation, and eventually passing. It is the object of our attention. We are the observer, the witness of the emotion.

The following dialogue between Ram Das (RD) and a person experiencing depression (DP) further illustrates this point.

> *DP: I'm depressed.*
>
> *RD: You're really depressed?*
>
> *DP: Yeah. I'm depressed.*
>
> *RD: You're completely depressed?*
>
> *DP: Yes, I'm completely depressed. Every bit of me. Oh boy am I depressed.*
>
> *RD: Oh! Any part of you not depressed?*
>
> *DP: No, completely depressed.*
>
> *RD: Are you noticing your depression?*

133

DP: Yes.

RD: Tell me - is the noticer depressed?

DP: Well, the noticer is just noticing.[3]

When you read the title of this chapter, you may have wondered, "Why is the final chapter of the book called 'Getting Started?'" This is the title that came to me. I will try to offer some explanation about why it is appropriate. The first reason is that we have not truly started living in this new paradigm until we begin experiencing the subtle shifts discussed in this chapter. We have laid the groundwork through prior chapters, and now we enter this subtle, yet powerful, transformation.

The second reason is that shifting to the new paradigm is not a one-time event. We fall back into the old, well-practiced paradigm. However, each time we come back to consciousness, it is a new beginning—we are once again *getting started*. It is presence now, not a continuation of the past. Consciousness only happens in the present moment.

So, we have come to the end of the invitation that is this book. You have been invited to join me in an experiment of living in this new paradigm—a paradigm in which we know ourselves as consciousness. We make this shift through an ongoing practice of witnessing our mind, emotions, and thoughts. My experience is that we may not notice the resulting changes at first. But, at certain points, we are amazed at how different our lives have become.

I am grateful for my teachers, for the teachings, and for you, my community.

About the Author

Marty Simon (Govind) is a retired professor of education living in the mountains of Colorado, where he enjoys skiing, hiking, and biking.

Since 1993, he has been a disciple of Yogi Amrit Desai and, for more than two decades, a grateful follower of Michael (Mickey) Singer. With over 15 years of experience leading meditation groups and sharing spiritual teachings, Marty currently leads an online meditation group that meets weekly—free and open to all.

Marty is available for interviews and as a guest teacher for groups and spiritual retreats and can be contacted by email at martinallensimon@gmail.com.

Notes

[1] https://www.ramdass.org/ram-dass-quotes/

[2] Quote taken from the webpage,
https://www.samwoolfe.com/2024/04/ram-dass-neuroses-shmoos.html.

[3] Becoming Nobody https://becomingnobody.com

www.ingramcontent.com/pod-product-compliance
Lightning Source LLC
Chambersburg PA
CBHW070938130626
46555CB00001B/488